FOIE GRAS, CAVIAR, SALMON & GOOSE IN THE RECIPES OF 31 GREAT CHEFS

BIBLIOTHECA CULINARIA

Art direction and graphic design: Tubello & Associati
Cover design: Dante Albieri
Photography: Janez Pukšič
Translation: Liz Marcucci Zazzera

© 2001 Jolanda de Colò S.r.l. with the title:
  Jolanda de Colò – Gli Artigiani del Gusto
© 2002 Bibliotheca Culinaria S.r.l. – 26900 Lodi, Italia
Tel. 0371-412684
Fax 0371-413287
e-mail: info@bibliothecaculinaria.it

ISBN 88-86174-37-3

October 2002

Foreword - Corrado Barberis
Preface - Carlo Petrini
Text - Bepi Pucciarelli
Photography - Janez Pukšič

FOREWORD

Why Pessot? Someday he will be credited with both preserving and renewing the patrimony of Italy's salumieri. In a world that has grown suspicious of pork-based products, he has opened an entirely new frontier by substituting the goose. In short, there is no creation without innovation. Legend has it that when the halcyons reached the limit of their endurance their wings were supported by those of their young apprentices. Extending the metaphor we might say that the interest aroused by Antonello Pessot's new products, from *prosciutto cotto d'oca* to *porcaloca*, is likely to help save such endangered "species" as the salami of San Benedetto, a specialty of Mantua cooked under a blanket of ashes. The rare Pietraroia prosciutto of Benevento might just take off as curiosity ferments around Pessot's leg of lamb or ostrich bresaola. And why not? Having made such a fine job of consolidating the artisanal know-how dispersed throughout the Friulian countryside, the "king" of geese can hardly be expected to limit his empire. Sheep, venison, salmon: they are all within his range. Not content with having made Friuli the production center for all goose related products, he has extended his gastronomical vision 360° or *tous azimuts* to use a phrase favored by De Gaulle. An old adage would have it that all that the eye beholds offers a constant reminder of the creator's presence. Without wanting to be sacrilegious, I'm tempted to say that whenever I sink my teeth into something new, I'm reminded of Antonello's presence. With the help of his lovely wife and his highly motivated son, he has created a company that seems to me a worthy heir of those French perfumers who are said to add champagne to their flacons in a quest for the ultimate in good taste.

Corrado Barberis
President, Italian Institute of Rural Sociology
INSOR

PREFACE

For many years (and long before the anti-globalization movement achieved visibility) Slow Food has engaged in a non-violent campaign against the standardization of modern eating habits.

I have written and spoken extensively on this subject, but I never tire of repeating that the real problem lies in the gulf that separates the two types of agricultural production. On the one hand rich multinational companies make low quality foodstuffs available to poor consumers through systems which enable them to make ample profits (hardly a laudable state of affairs, but certainly a more acceptable one if it really did constitute an advance against world hunger). This is countered by the comparatively "poor" agriculture that produces small quantities of high-quality foods (often in danger of extinction) for the niche markets created by well-heeled consumers – a category which often fails to attribute the correct value to the products themselves or the intense labor which was required to produce them.

Slow Food's goal, as evidenced by its creation of the Ark for endangered foodstuffs, its Presìdi, its defense of unpasteurized cheeses and many other initiatives, is not only that of making people aware of the value of artisanal foodstuffs but also of the labor which lies behind them. If asked to cite an example that proves our efforts should not be dismissed as utopian, Antonello Pessot's name is one that immediately springs to mind.

He has called himself a craftsman of flavor. This seems a reductive definition, given his entrepreneurial flair, yet it is a useful one for its allusion to the very real dividing line which exists between industrial production (where human intervention is relegated to set up and control) and that where intelligence, sensibility, creativity and manual dexterity play their parts in every single item produced. Antonello Pessot is something more than a craftsman of flavor. I think of him more as a talent scout for endangered foods.

There is an element of irony in his story, which began with the goose, or more precisely with foie gras. When his adventures in the gastronomical world got underway nearly thirty years ago it could hardly be considered a threatened product. Today, it risks becoming outlawed.

Still, I think talent scout is the right term, even if his research does have a well-defined purpose: the enrichment of his catalogue of specialties. His philosophy is that of an illuminated entrepreneur. If a given foodstuff lacks even the most basic production structure, but he perceives a demand (real or potential) for it, then there is a market space to be filled and someone has to do it.

There is, of course, sound business sense behind this. When he departs from traditional products like *sasaka* or *pitina* and by reelaborating their recipes succeeds in making them known beyond their home base, this creates additional interest and demand. Aside from these incursions into the realm of endangered Friulian specialties or adventurous expeditions to locate the finest salmon or sturgeon, Antonello Pessot's name, like that of his wife Jolanda De Colo, is inextricably tied to the goose and the many gastronomical delights it supplies.

There is perhaps a grain of truth to the assertion that Brillat Savarin is the father of modern gastronomy and in seconding this I believe I'm being objective and not partisan. Still, I was forced to revise my opinion at least once

when years ago during one of Arcigola's first events in Pessot territory, I discovered foie gras "made in Friuli." Here was a product that our cousins on the other side of the Alps could only envy.

Antonello and his family not only succeeded in changing my opinion regarding foie gras, they astonished me with their foie gras al Picolit, a fine invention and a marvelous intuition. More than the product of the fervid imagination of an artisan, this was an artist's work of genius.

There is a much-abused aphorism of Brillat Savarin that compares the invention of a new dish to the discovery of a new star. While Jolanda De Colo's products can be said to represent a veritable constellation in the gastronomical heavens, foie gras al Picolit shines like a supernova.

Carlo Petrini
President, International Slow Food Movement

THE FANTASTIC STORY OF THE WHITE GOOSE

There are people, events and places which have the power to remind us of a common history, a shared past – fragments of nursery rhymes memorized long ago, pieces of fables and legends which remain fixed in our minds. All Italians recall the story of the geese of the Capitol who saved Rome from the Barbarians with their strident warning cries. Through this account the goose makes one of its earliest appearances in Western legend, yet somehow it never managed to achieve the same prominence as other less likable birds. The owl, for example, has become a symbol of wisdom with its piercing gaze penetrating the darkness of ignorance and lighting the way for philosophers. So, what has the goose come to represent? Can its iconographic innocence be construed as symbolic of the simple and bucolic – neither bad-tempered nor intriguing – but certainly practical and down to earth? Left to patrol the barnyard, the poor goose has become associated with a disappearing way of life, one that has gradually faded over the course of the twentieth century as a forced modernization has supplanted our ties to all things rural.

The goose really does seem the proper emblem of homespun wisdom, of our ties to the land and our most wholesome sentiments. Its gait is hardly elegant; it passes most of its time napping between meals and if left to its own devices it, will stuff itself with its favorite food, yet there is something very appealing about the goose. Its easy-going affability and the trust it so naturally extends to its human caretakers seem to tell us how seriously the goose takes its status as a domesticated animal. Of course, there are those who say that the goose is noisy, gluttonous and nosy, but there's no denying that its gaze betrays a sort of subtle intelligence.

Italy's popular board game, the gioco dell'oca or goose game is often said to mirror the game of life. With its triumphs and tricks, its reversals and inevitable march to the finish, it offers a range of experiences to all players.

Talking about Jolanda de Colò without talking about the goose is simply impossible. The company's voyage of discovery, which has hardly begun to catalogue all of the finds within its range, began with its rediscovery of this animal. Jolanda de Colò's history might best be represented as a goose game come to life, one which extends over time with few interruptions, one with no missed turns and one where the finish line is nowhere in sight. This game was set in motion by the drive and energy of its two principal players and they were soon joined by a third contender, one equally adept at running the course. Two players, two families; two different ways of approaching the game, of taking each lap, but with a single goal – that of creating a new approach to food, one which would recover real flavors and give a proper sense of importance to gastronomical culture.

In a narrative, character description is at best difficult and often irrelevant because, in most instances, actions are far more eloquent than mere profiles. In the case of Jolanda de Colò and its protagonists, Antonello Pessot, Alana Jolanda de Colò and their son Bruno, their stories unfold in such a way that events, successes, and personal histories may be seen to be all of a piece with the personalities which set them in motion. To a large extent, their stories tell themselves and like the best narratives they have tightly constructed plots with plenty of action and not a few surprises.

My protagonists have very different personalities, but I find myself instinctively beginning with Antonello Pessot, perhaps because his exuberance, curiosity and easy-going manner won me over. His story is a long one, but an amusing one to unravel, full of the vicissitudes of life as it is really lived, of anecdotes, of vitality and creativity.

In the Pessot family, the roles are well defined and Antonello is the creative force. Strong and determined, Alana de Colò is a woman whose organizational and managerial skills are capable of turning her husband's ideas into reality. Under her direction, everyone associated with the business makes his best effort and this has always been so, from the time that Jolanda de Colò became Italy's leading producer of geese for the table to the time when it expanded its range and the Pessots began researching and selecting delicacies from around the world in order to offer them to the country's finest restaurants. Her presence today is as essential as it was at the outset. Jolanda de Colò without Alana's decisiveness is simply unthinkable. Bruno Pessot joined the family firm upon completing his studies in business administration and soon demonstrated that he was well suited to the role of young entrepreneur. Imbued with the family passion for fine food, he has directed his considerable energies to research and development. After all, his doctoral thesis concerned foie gras. Today Bruno directs the company with a spontaneous even-handedness that is the fruit of the creative evolution of his parents. His attentiveness has predisposed the company for significant future growth. While it may seem odd to speak of a business in these terms, in Northeastern Italy such family activities are so much a part of the personalities which created them that the dividing line is often obscure and one never quite knows where the physical subject ends and the economic concern begins.

Alana Jolanda de Colò created the first Jolanda de Colò in 1976. An agricultural concern, it was dedicated to raising geese for their meat and livers. Over the years its evolution followed that of its creators who became increasingly interested in furnishing restaurants with the high quality ingredients essential to haute cuisine. Today the company headquarters is located just outside of Palmanova and it shares something of the city's history in the concept which underlies its founding.

When the Venetian Republic decided to construct an impenetrable military blockade against the advance of the Turks, it chose the Friulian plain as the most suitable site for this fortified city. Palmanova was built using the most advanced technology of the time in terms of weaponry and defense. Its founders reasoned that should the Turks decide to attack Venice by land, they would have to pass this point, cross the Gorizia pass and dash across the plain devastating the entire region, precisely as they did two centuries earlier. The finest engineers and architects were summoned to construct the city's star-shaped walled perimeter and its internal structures. Their efforts produced one of the world's finest examples of military architecture. That it has remained intact to the present day is perhaps one of the most significant testimonies to the power of the lion of St. Mark. Fortunately, the city never hosted a battle. The cannons and bombs that figured so prominently in the imagination of its founders never marred its architectural splendor. Palmanova was conceived as a fortified outpost against Ottoman barbarism just as Jolanda de Colò may be considered a bulwark against the invasion represented by the standardization of contemporary eating habits. We can only hope that it persists in its mission as efficiently as the magnificent star-shaped city.

Still, my protagonists beckon as does the heart of their story and I must allow each his part. Antonello quite naturally assumes the role of greeting all of Jolanda de Colò's visitors and I'm sure I was not the only one who noticed his very mobile, expressive eyes. Flashing blue with each turn of his story, they sometimes seemed to betray

his difficulty in keeping his creative energy in check. I found Antonello's account of the company's challenging early days particularly interesting. There were times when he rose at 4:00 a.m. to personally check the freshness of shipments arriving from abroad, but these tasks were soon accompanied by more pleasant ones: encounters with talented chefs and journalists who were truly interested in the burgeoning market for gourmet foods. Their appreciation for his efforts was very gratifying.

The attention Antonello reserves for his merchandise is not unlike that of a jeweler. Present production methods are the end results of years of research. He has continually attempted to understand the factors behind the origin of each product by departing from their most quotidian uses, from the richness implicit in everyday things that so often eludes us. When describing the traditional methods of herdsmen from the Valcellina, Antonello makes their hardships, their nights under the stars, the lonely mountain panorama which surround them, very real. By joining the flavors produced by such a life with a very modern spirit of conservation, he has succeeded in offering us not only a delicious product, but one that has the additional cachet of having been saved from the grasp of oblivion.

After listening to Antonello, I had the vague sensation that I was perhaps savoring his tale more so than the product he was so meticulously describing. It was a bit like finding oneself privy to the personality quirks of a great chef or the know-how of one of the Piedmont's master salumai without ever having met them or even seen their photographs. I came to the uncanny realization that in this business, as in the theater, there is much to be said for the evocative power of the underlying story.

Antonello has a counterpart. Like many successful creative people he supported by a practical figure who balances his artistic personality and finds rational ways of putting his ideas to work. Alana very discretely fills this important role. She has a cool, composed way of dealing with all of those material things that interpose themselves between her husband's inventiveness and business necessity. Alana has always been the motive force behind the day-to-day business of Jolanda de Colò. She has navigated with a steady hand and her prowess has grown with time. Her decision, over thirty years ago, to concentrate the company's efforts on geese ran counter to mainstream marketing logic. Consumers were becoming intrigued by luxury foods, by more exotic offerings. The familiar barnyard figure that had long been a fixture of local, home cooking hardly fit this image. Yet, Alana persisted with courage and determination. It was her tenacity that allowed the business to grow. It was her determination that transformed Jolanda de Colò into the prime mover on the new front of safeguarding tradition.

In the meantime, Antonello was learning the ropes of agribusiness, experimenting with new forms of management, new products and innovative solutions while managing a large farm for absent owners. While Alana was pushing ahead in silence surrounded by her geese in the seemingly endless fields of Lower Friuli, Antonello was seeking new markets and new goals. Fortunately, the farsightedness of his employers allowed him to experiment and he was able to discover (long before it became a media issue) that there were still consumers who categorically refused standardized tastes, uniform flavors. Thirty years ahead of the pack, Antonello began his private war against the "plastic" flavors and pre-packaged foods that taste the same from Buenos Aires to Bologna. He was motivated by the conviction that gustatory freedom contributes to intellectual freedom. Only by returning to original flavors and by safeguarding local agricultural practices with all of their idiosyncrasies can we preserve the diversity that is essential to giving things "human" and not industrial characteristics. Today, many have come to the realization that the real gastronomic revolution lies in freeing food from the standardization that modern industrial methods have forced upon it.

As often occurs, the company's growth has been marked by its owners' encounters with extraordinary people who influenced them on a personal level. Toward the end of the 1970s Antonello met Luciano Curiel, a butcher with a shop in Venice. He turned out to be the city's last guardian of the ritual method of butchering geese according to Hebrew tradition and the custodian of a recipe for kosher goose salami. His effect on Antonello was enormous. Not only did Luciano teach him a great deal about his trade, he did this in the best oral tradition. The account of his long experience was spun out like a magical tale, revealing its teller to be at once simple and profound. Driven by his desire to bring this man's knowledge to a wider audience, Antonello became even more committed to discovering the basic know-how underlying the seemingly infinite regional variants of Italy's many traditional preserved meats. No stranger to fine food (his family had run a small restaurant in the hills outside Conegliano Veneto since 1860), Antonello was now discovering the possibility of bringing this kind of regional cuisine to a whole new audience. The fine points of taste need no longer be associated only with French food or luxury restaurants and their self-involved culture. Great flavors, extraordinary tastes were just as much a part of Italian regional cuisine and the rural culture that had preserved it. They simply hadn't been proposed in the best way. His friendship with Luciano Curial brought Antonello to the understanding that variety conserved through tradition in the country's farmyards was, in fact, a hidden resource. He began to see those geese Alana had persisted in raising in a totally different light.

The goose's silhouette, which serves as Jolanda de Colò's logo, may be seen as a sentinel, a guard against standardized flavors, against imitation, against the blandness of the supermarket world and all it represents, but this was yet to come. Antonello's new found commitment needed to manifest itself in concrete way. His first step on the road to consolidating his mission was the founding of the Fattoria del Oca Bianca or White Goose Farm in 1987. In its name he traveled throughout Italy and abroad in search of the artisanal foodstuffs that met his stiff criteria in terms of respecting tradition and quality control. Soon many of Italy's top restaurants were turning to him for the unusual or long forgotten delicacies he had brought to light. They began to use his considerable skills as a talent scout for tracking down all of the things that had been relegated to the category of gastronomic myth. And he satisfied them. Perpetually booked on the next flight out, he was relentlessly on the trail and just as relentlessly he brought his treasures home. It was an exciting way of life, but a tiring one. Always on the run from one quality control session to the next and buffeted by the growing avidity of suppliers who, until they met him, had never hoped to see their products on the tables of Italy's top restaurants, he began to feel the effects of such a frenetic pace. He found himself checking in with his customers from further and further away. Convinced that he could find anything, chefs began asking him for the impossible. It was evident that the White Goose Farm would have to be, if not abandoned, at least transformed.

The situation presented a new challenge. Alana's business had been growing steadily. Her cottage industry had been transformed into an economically solid concern. Why not see how far it could go? Could it conceivably become another of Northeastern Italy's entrepreneurial success stories? The time had arrived for Antonello and Alana to join forces, to take on a common objective. Experience had consolidated their views. Through the White Goose Farm Antonello had gained the confidence of Italy's most elite restauranteurs and their most talented chefs. These contacts existed and he need only develop them, while maintaining the format that had worked so well for White Goose

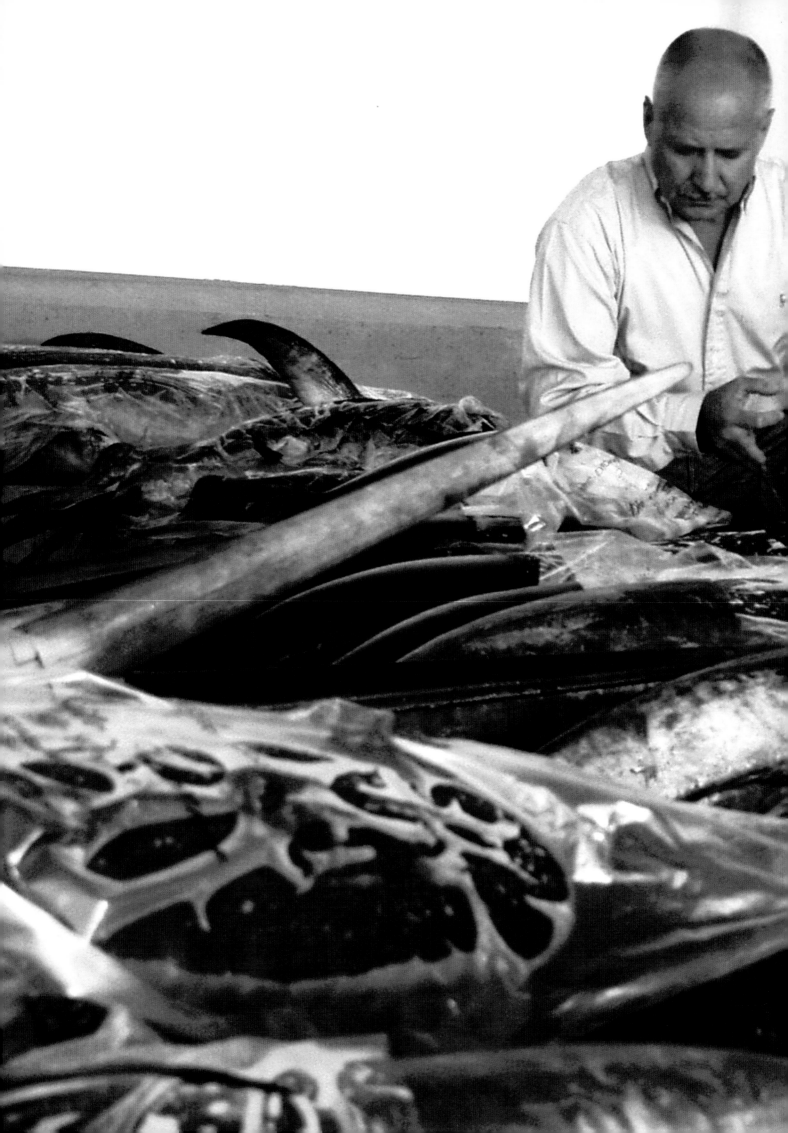

Farm. Antonello and Alana pooled their human resources – contacts, friends, friends of friends – to create the Jolanda de Colò we know today, an industry leader. Antonello could count on his very justified reputation as a "defender of the rural world" given that no less than Corrado Barberis, president of Italy's National Institute for Rural Sociology had granted him this honorific. Because the title was certainly one he had earned, it was no leap for Jolanda de Colò's logo to become associated with "saved products." Over the years it has continually renewed its founders commitment to this kind of activity by rediscovering and reproducing dozens of products that were slated for extinction. Antonello has placed day-to-day operations in the able hands of his son Bruno and this has freed him to return to his first love, an ongoing search for great artisanal foods produced on a local level.

The original inspiration provided by the goose has led the Pessots to other sectors of the fine food market, from specialty meats to fish to caviar. Antonello continues to rely on great chefs for their input and advice. As operators on the gastronomic front line, their opinions are important, not only with respect to new trends, but also in terms

of that all-important link to the past. He is proud of having acquired their trust and hopes that he has returned to them as much as they have given him.

Every Jolanda de Colò employee learns about the products he helps to create, their history, their evolution, what gives them their distinctive flavor and the necessity of maintaining that precious aspect over time. Their efforts have contributed to making the company name a guarantee for the best. They can be seen as having joined the Pessots in their battle against gastronomic standardization and all that it implies. We can only hope that they represent the vanguard of a larger movement that will one day definitively eliminate the possibility that everything tastes the same.

Bepi Pucciarelli

FOIE GRAS

GOOSE FOIE GRAS

TRADITION MAKES FOR A REFINED TABLE

The goose's potential for supplying foie gras was known in remote times, but it was the Romans who raised the dish to the level of the sublime. Yet, in Italy during the Middle Ages production all but disappeared, reemerging only later by way of French gastronomic tradition.

Prior to migration, wild geese feed abundantly causing a natural enlargement of the liver. With the correct diet, it is possible to reproduce this alteration, transforming the liver into foie gras.

In accordance with long-standing rural tradition, Jolanda De Colo raises its geese in small groups of ten to twenty, allowing them to range freely in the uncontaminated fields of its Hungarian reserves. The birds, carefully monitored by local experts, are butchered according to rigorously set procedures. Only the finest livers, selected by professionals, are then destined for sale as foie gras.

VINICIO DOVIER: TWO-STAR CATERING

Dovier earned his two Michelin stars in the1980s as chef of the famous Boschetti restaurant in Tricesimo. It was there that he spent the greater part of his professional career and there that he brought international acclaim to the cuisine of his native Friuli (and particularly that of Grado). With his protégé Romeo Sturma, in 1994 Dovier inaugurated an ambitious venture: Viroca (Vinicio and Romeo Catering). Representing the best in catering in the Friuli Venezia Giulia region, it is capable of serving from two to two thousand with unwavering quality and an attention to details - from the linens to the silver to the wine selection – all of which are on par with Viroca's truly exceptional cuisine.

DUCK FOIE GRAS

THE DISTINCTIVE FLAVOR OF DUCK FOIE GRAS

Duck foie gras is produced in a manner similar to that of goose foie gras, but it does present some distinguishing characteristics. Less delicate than that of goose foie gras, its flavor is stronger and more decisive. From a visual point of view as well, the two types of liver are easily distinguished. While goose foie gras commonly presents two nearly symmetrical lobes, duck foie gras is composed of one larger lobe and one smaller one. It is usually yellowish in color with a pink cast while goose foie gras tends toward a light gray tone.

MAXIM - THE UNMISTAKABLE ARCHITECTURE OF FLAVORS

In the Fifties and Sixties a boom in modernist architecture seemed destined to imperil the Mitteleuropean beauty of the Slovenian city of Ljubljana. Perhaps by coincidence or perhaps as a challenge, one of the finest restaurants of the region, Maxim, is located in one of these newer buildings. Slavko Adamlje, the chef of this 'cult' gastronomic destination was for years a pupil of Bocuse and he certainly assimilated the master's touch. His restaurant offers typical Slovenian cuisine, enhanced by cooking techniques that are clearly French in origin. Though considered one of the most knowledgeable and nuanced interpreters of foie gras, Adamlje allows his haute cuisine to coexist with such local specialties as the hand-cut baked ham served with horseradish.

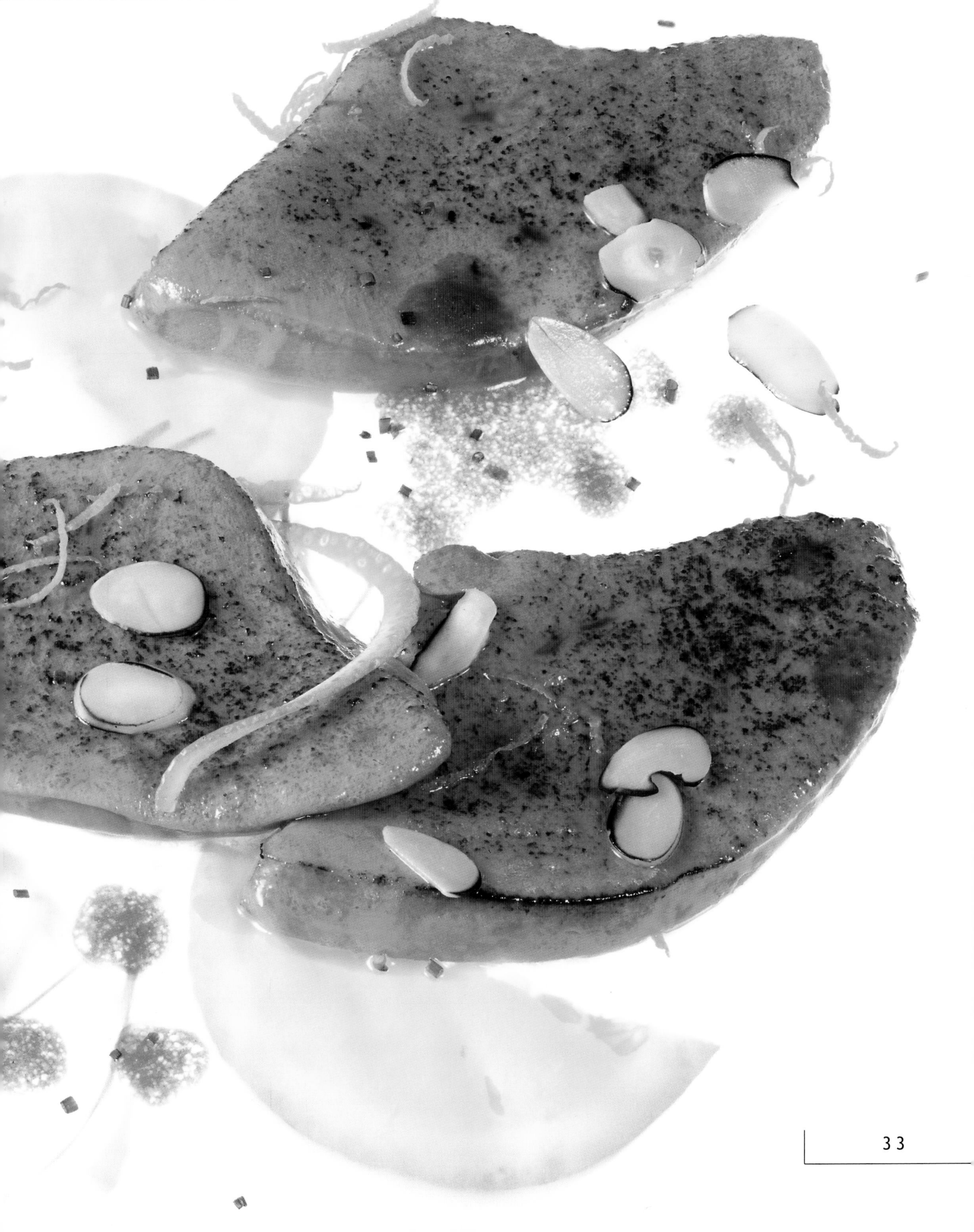

GOOSE FOIE GRAS

THE MARRIAGE OF FISH AND FOIE GRAS

Magic in the kitchen: the only possible definition for goose foie gras as an enhancement to the flavor of fish, especially whitefish. Found in the lakes of Switzerland, Austria and Northern Italy, this long, tapered, white-fleshed salmonoid with its particularly subtle flavor becomes a true delicacy in the hands of Riccardo De Pra. His artistry lay in identifying precisely which element could serve to meld the two flavors. The Straol potato, which flourishes in dry, mineral-rich soil, is a firm-fleshed, starchy tuber with an ivory color. The sauce (or perhaps more correctly, the broth) derived from cooking these potatoes with the fish is then used to heat the combined ingredients to great effect. A smooth, slightly acidic white wine, such as a Tokaji from Friuli makes the perfect accompaniment.

A CENTURIES-OLD TRADITION

Elegant, intimate, radiating class – these are the salient characteristics of Dolada in Plois di Pieve d'Alpago in the province of Belluno. The restaurant has remained in the De Prà family for four generations with Enzo and Rossana De Prà presently at the helm, assisted by their children Riccardo and Benedetta. Only the highest quality ingredients, gleaned from a meticulous search among local purveyors make their way into its kitchen. Dolada has something to offer a wide range of diners, from the traveler lured by its more creative cuisine to the locals in search of traditional fare.

It offers a rich wine list, which exhibits particular depth with regard to whites from Friuli, reds from Tuscany and the Piedmont and the autochthonous production of Sicily. Its over six hundred wines are personally selected by Rossana (a professional sommelier) who presides over the dining room with her daughter. Internationally trained Enzo De Prà reigns in the kitchen, ably assisted by his son whose recent apprenticeships have taken him from England to Belgium to Japan.

SMOKED GOOSE FOIE GRAS

ANCIENT FLAVORS FOR THE PALATE'S PLEASURE

Smoked foie gras cannot properly said to be "cooked," otherwise it would loose both its original flavor and its characteristic texture. Only the finest, premium quality foie gras may be destined for smoking. With great care the selected livers are deveined, lightly salted and spiced according to Jolanda De Colo's recipe, which was developed so as not to mask the product's essential nature. At this point the livers are 'cold-smoked': exposed to the tepid fumes of burning beech wood, juniper and other spices. Through this process, which is closer to pasteurization than to cooking, the foie gras conserves its original flavor.

THE GOLDEN EAGLE OF THE FRIULIAN HILLS

What could lie behind the walls of a castle whose windows frame both the rolling hills of Eastern Friuli, gently declining towards Slovenia and (on a clear, sunny day) the sea? Nothing less than one of the region's 'jewels', the restaurant that is most often cited as a source of local pride. In this enchanted site, Anna and Giorgio Tuti welcome their guests to beautifully decorated rooms where every single detail, from the china to the silverware to the glassware, has been selected with care. Their goal is simply to offer the best and this is reflected in the service as well. Quiet and reserved, Giorgio is the emblematic figure of the castle and it is he who looks after the dining room while Anna releases her creative energy in the kitchen. Each year she follows a course of specialization in Australia, a country she has come to love. "There I can discover all sorts of flavors and techniques which are not available to me in this far corner of Italy."

GOOSE FOIE GRAS

THE DELICIOUS COMBINATION OF FOIE GRAS AND BLACK TRUFFLES

Through the centuries foie gras – the liver of fattened geese - has achieved and consolidated a mythic status in international culinary circles. Every chef of note has his own variation on the theme. With his use of this important De Colo product, Alessandro Scian seeks to surprise. His version of the classic terrine employs spices and the black, summer season truffles from Acqualagna. He serves this delicious combination with a spicy marmalade made from apples and red grapefruit and accompanies it with slices of homemade brioche. This sweet and delicate dish demands a prestigious wine. At La Taverna it is paired with a French Sauternes.

AGE-OLD TRADITION FOR LIGHT, MODERN CUISINE

Pietro Zanini and Vinicio Sant are better termed the guiding spirits than the proprietors of La Taverna in Colloredo di Monte Albano. For quite some time they have chosen to offer traditional Friulian cuisine tempered by a lighter, more modern approach. The dishes prepared with the goose offer perhaps the best example of this successful blending of old and new. Chef Scian commands a fine brigade and the restaurant (set just across from the Nievo castle) is fortunately situated in one of the most beautiful parts of Friuli on one of the first Morainic hills a few kilometers outside of Udine. Having held a Michelin star for years, the restaurant boasts a refined, international clientele. It wine list offers a vast selection of the world's finest vintages represented by over 1,200 labels in over 40,000 bottles, all of which are held a large cellar situated over an antique well over 30 meters deep.

STUFFED BREAST OF GOOSE

THE PERFECT BALANCE OF FLAVOR AND GOOD TASTE

Breast of goose stuffed with foie gras is one of the most elegant of Jolanda di Colo's products. Tender goose breast is paired with delicate foie gras (seasoned with salt, pepper, spices and a blend of spirits) and then gently steamed resulting in a perfect symbiosis of flavors and textures. Ida Tondolo, the chef of Là di Petros has interpreted this ingredient with classic simplicity: thin slices of the stuffed goose breast are dressed with a few drops of balsamic vinegar and served on grape leaves accompanied by a small bunch of white grapes cooked in Verduzzo wine. When the season does not permit a garnish of grape leaves she substitutes with a salad of tender baby greens similarly dressed in balsamic vinegar. With lightly toasted bread and a glass of Verduzzo Friulano passito, the dish is complete.

GUSTATORY HARMONY AND A LIGHT TOUCH

Là di Petros is located in the Mels quarter of Colloredo di Monte Albano and is home to one of the best mixes of enogastronomical talent in Friuli. The reserved Ida Tondolo commands the kitchen. Though largely self-taught she exhibits the solid professionalism acquired through years of experience. Just after the earthquake of 1976, she began refining her culinary skills, eventually perfecting them in France where she assimilated the Gallic dexterity for using every ingredient which nature offers to its fullest potential, wasting nothing. Her husband, Liano Petrozzi presides over the dining room and the cellar (10,000 bottles representing 500 wines) with a winning blend of competence and affability. Their restaurant is small and well appointed in every detail, offering up to 45 diners a sense of intimacy and privacy. Two cardinal rules govern the establishment: the utmost importance is granted to balancing flavors – no single element should assert itself above the others and all diners must leave the restaurant with their appetite satisfied though not weighted down by the cuisine.

CLASSIC TERRINE OF FOIE GRAS

SIMPLE AND DELICATE – FOIE GRAS IN TERRINE

The gourmand can enjoy foie gras in many forms and while each has its merits and may be suited to different occasions, perhaps the basic terrine offers the refined palate the most simple and direct way of appreciating this delicate ingredient. For its terrines Jolanda De Colo uses only the finest goose livers selected from free ranging geese raised in its Hungarian reserves. After being carefully deveined the whole lobes are delicately salted, spiced and then enclosed in the classic hermetically sealed jars in which they are briefly cooked. Prior to being transferred to tins, the livers are then marinated so as to conserve their aromas and unmistakable flavor.

ENOGASTRONOMY FOR GOURMETS

A family tradition for dedicating one's energies to the gourmet sector (restaurants, delicatessens, the coffee trade) provided Luigi Damiani and his wife Lidia with the proper background for opening a small, exclusive wine shop. Represented by nearly 1000 labels divided among the best domestic production as well as imports from France, California and the emerging nations such as Chile, wine represents the focus of the Damianis' activity. In addition to the fine vintages from around the world, they offer an equally refined selection of specialized foods of the highest quality: cheeses, salumi, oils, vinegars and sweets. All of these were chosen with an eye toward their discerning clientele who enjoy giving the best to others (and to themselves).

TORCHON OF FOIE GRAS

THE FINEST FOIE GRAS FOR A TRULY SPECIAL PRODUCT

The unmistakable flavor of foie gras perhaps achieves its best expression when prepared in torchon. Jolanda De Colo's version employs the finest unbroken lobes. These are deveined, salted, spiced and then allowed to soak for several hours in milk. With great artistry the two lobes are then repositioned in their original interlocking fashion so as to form a nearly perfect cylinder. Wrapped in a cloth (hence the name from the French *torchon*) each is then slightly compressed and then briefly cooked by steaming at a low temperature.

TRADITION RENEWED

With time some things leave their mark on the natural world and on its human inhabitants. Such is the case with the cuisine of Gianni Cosetti, the great chef of Tolmezzo's Roma restaurant. His protégé, Daniele Cortiula, is now chef-proprietor at the Kursaal in Sauris. There diners may discover not only an unforgettable tiny mountain village whose inhabitants are descended from Northern Germany, but also by warm hospitality, exceptional cuisine and fine wines. Cortiula's cooking reflects local tradition and ingredients in much the same way that his mentor's did, with masterful touches and great expressivity. His Toc' in braide is an excellent example. This polenta-based dish (originally re-elaborated by Cosetti) is prepared at Kursaal in the most exclusive of versions – with foie gras.

FOIE GRAS

PROTAGONIST: FOIE GRAS

Ficatum was the name the ancient Romans gave to the liver of a goose raised on figs. The technique of force feeding was not only well-known to them, it was also widely diffused throughout the Empire. Even after the linguistic passage from Latin to Italian, the term *ficatum* persisted and became synonymous with liver. Thanks to Jewish tradition, the technique survived the Middle Ages. In Hungary, in France and in Italy, Jewish communities preserved the time honored method for fattening geese. The French predilection for foie gras is amply documented. Particularly favored by the French Kings and their famous chefs, *pâté de foie gras en croute* is said to have been perfected for Louis XVI. Foie gras was certainly regal fare, but it was no less appreciated by artists. George Sand, Alexander Dumas and Gioacchino Rossini were great admirers of this delicacy with latter's "tournedos" being perhaps as much appreciated as his operas.

GERMANY'S GIFT TO ROME - A GREAT CHEF

If the geese which warned the Romans of the Gallic invasion in 387 B.C. were most likely auctochthonous, in succeeding years the Romans began importing geese which were fattened to perfection by their Germanic neighbors. Whether this represented a kind of globalization ante litteram or an Italo-Germanic culinary axis remains to be established. Nevertheless, the exchange has been repeated twenty centuries later and to great advantage. Instead of geese, the Romans have adopted a top chef. Heinz Beck (the guiding force behind the city's top restaurant La Pergola), arrived in 1994 with a star-studded curriculum. Having logged experience in the kitchens of Berlin's Harlekin and Monaco's Tantris, he went on to work with both Heinz Winkler and Alfred Klink to refine his technique. The cuisine he proposes in Rome is continually evolving, but is distinguished by its lightness and its preference for decidedly Mediterranean flavors. In his recently published cookbook Beck has defined his mission: "I am always searching for new combinations of flavors and textures, new solutions and surprises which respect both the local cuisine and Italy's cultural heritage."

FOIE GRAS

By Land, by sea and by Air

We have become accustomed to thinking of the goose as a farmyard animal and this is largely true given that archeological sites in northern and central Europe have offered traces of its domestication dating from thousands of years ago. Yet before domestication (or in the case of wild species), the goose used its powerful wings for long range flight, covering incredible distances in its yearly migratory cycle. Despite its webbed feet and its ability to swim, the goose is not classified as an aquatic bird, like the duck or the swan. Still, the goose is equally comfortable on land, in the water or in the air and this versatility is mirrored in its gastronomic uses. Foie gras, in particular lends itself to many different transformations and combinations with other flavors.

Between Sky and Sea...

The Locanda delle Tamerici is located in Ameglia (SP), at the southernmost point of the province of Liguria which borders on Tuscany. It takes its name from the tamarisk trees which surround its garden, a tiny green oasis that separates the inn from its own private beach. This is beautifully tended, like the rest of the complex from the rooms to the outdoor dining area, from the main dining room to the cozy sitting room. Service, decor, and of course cuisine, follow suit. The proprietor, Mauro Ricciardi, commands the kitchen and in only a few years this self-taught chef has succeeded in winning the praise of not only the Italian fine dining guides, but has also earned a Michelin star. He attributes the latter in great part to his wife Bruna whose vigilance in the dining room is legendary. Ricciardi proposes creative cuisine with an emphasis on seafood. Yet, a personal predilection for foie gras is revealed in the many suggestive dishes which grace his menu throughout the year: *Lobster stuffed with foie gras in honey sauce, Colonnata lard wrapped monkfish on foie gras sauce* and the splendid *Salad of mixed baby greens with foie gras and broiled shrimp.*

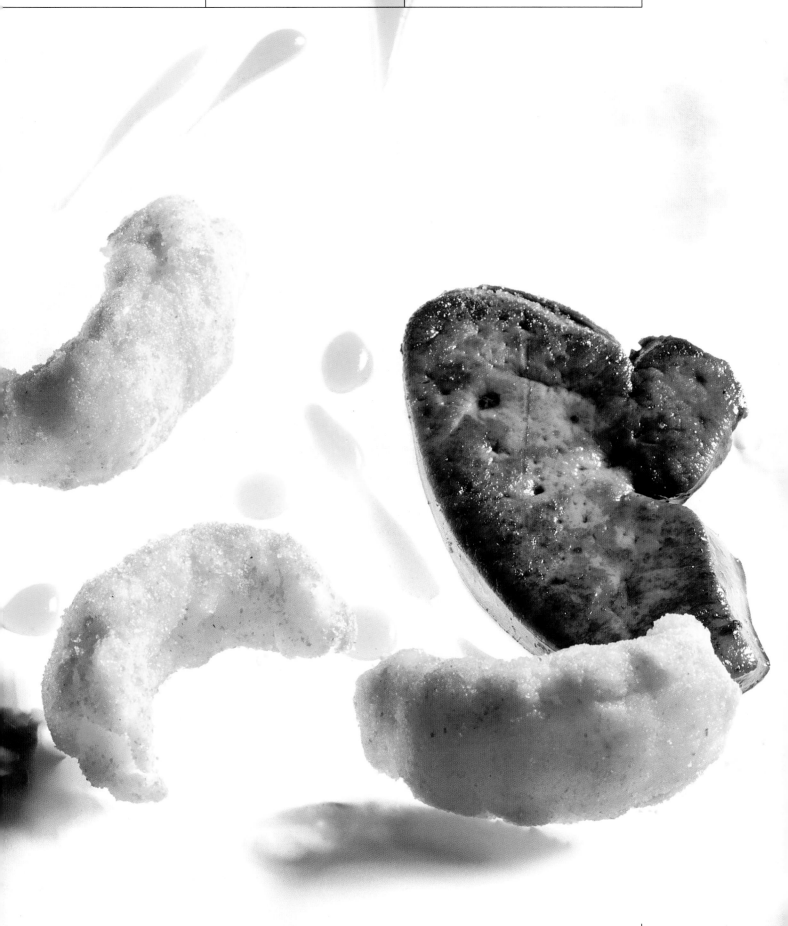

GOOSE FOIE GRAS

CAFFÈ FLORIAN - WHERE FOIE GRAS IS AN ART

The Venetians have called Saint Mark's Square the world's most beautiful sitting room and the Caffè Florian is one of its most essential elements. There is art in the air at the Florian – in its richly decorated 18th century decor; in its history (the Venice Biennale was conceived there at the end of the 19th century); in its contemporary involvement in cultural events; in the daily concerts it offers from April to October and certainly in the sense of the art of good living which has been practiced there for nearly three centuries. In this atmosphere it is only natural that foie gras should achieve the status of art as well. Florian's singular version is the result of collaboration between its executive chef Angelo Ruatti and a master of artisanal gelato, Erminio Largaiolli. Their brainchild includes four variations on the theme: scallops of fresh foie gras, foie gras sauce, ice cream made from smoked foie gras and a final decorative touch: smoked foie gras curls.

TO FLORIAN

"Let's go to the Florian." Venetians began repeating this popular refrain as early as 1720 when Floriano Francesconi first opened his café. Though originally named *Venice Triumphs*, this never caught on with the public who insisted on the name *Caffè Florian,* which has survived to the present day. Over 700,000 visitors from all over the world pass through its six rooms and terrace in the course of each year. Here Venetian regulars and Japanese tourists rub elbows with celebrities and jet setters as they enjoy a coffee, an aperitif, a light lunch or more substantial fare. Yet, even the most casual observer can detect the additional allure of this historic café whose glorious history includes an incredible roster of Italian clients - Giacomo Casanova, Carlo Goldoni, Giuseppe Parini, Silvio Pellico, Niccolò Tommaseo, Ugo Foscollo, Gabriele D'Annunzio, Eleonora Duse – and an equally illustrious list of international luminaries: Lord Byron, Goethe, Madame de Stael, Charles Dickens, Marcel Proust, Jean-Jacques Rousseau, Igor Stravinsky, Arthur Rubenstein.

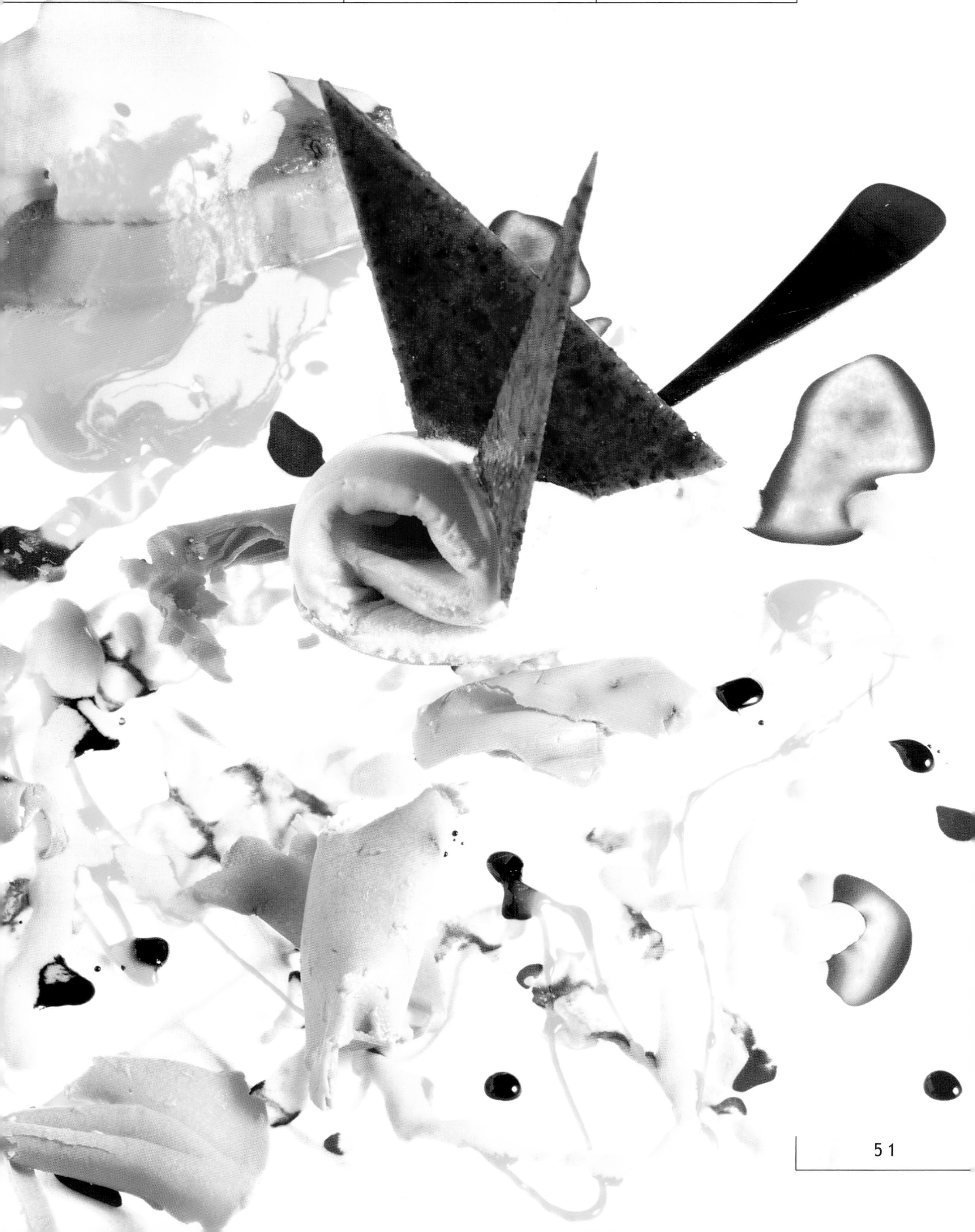

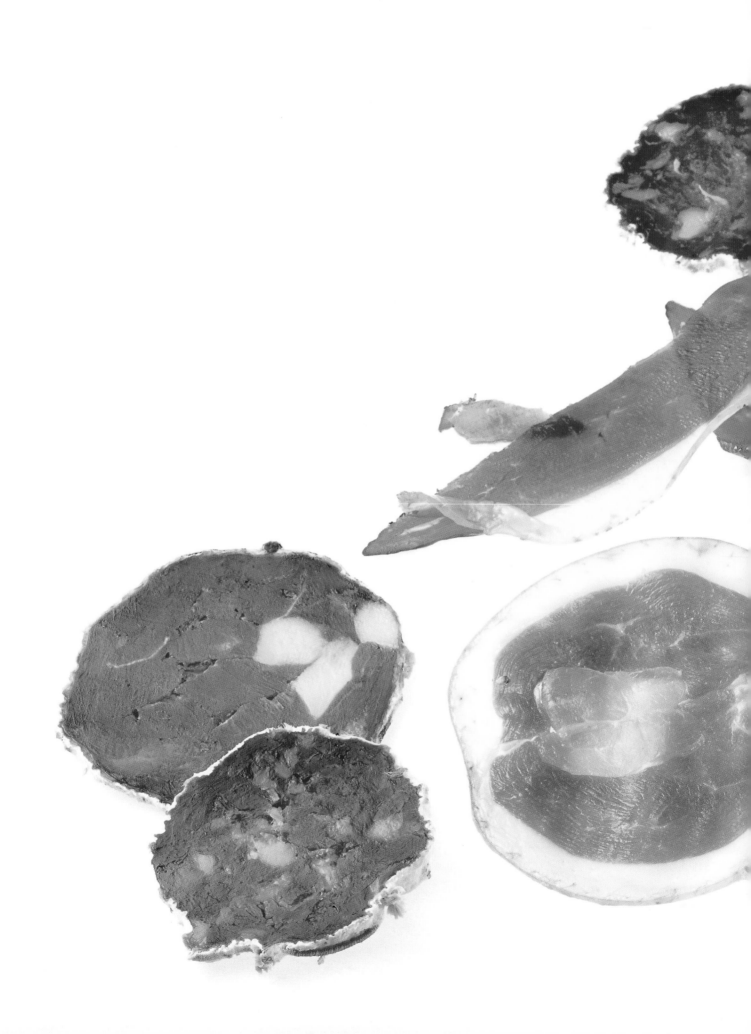

Rolled Goose Breast

Selected meats smoked over juniper and laurel

Rolled goose breast has been one of Jolanda De Colo's best sellers for over twenty-five years. It is prepared with Toulouse geese (the preferred breed for meat and liver production) that are nourished exclusively on grass and corn throughout their entire breeding cycle. Jolanda De Colo's geese are allowed to range freely for six months and in the final twenty days of their nutrition program they are segregated and fed only corn.

The two lobes of breast meat are detached from the bone, leaving the skin intact which unites them and makes it possible to give the product its compact, rolled shape. The rolled breasts are subjected to careful, cold smoking that traditionally employs the aromas from buring beech wood, oak, juniper berries and bay leaves.

Quality of Life in the Simple Flavors

The atmosphere is that of a workingman's club. Among the tables, simply prepared for the noon meal, one can still find the occasional retired streetcar operator playing cards and enjoying a glass of wine. In the evening, along with traditional Lombard fare, the restaurant offers a wide range of original dishes and an extraordinary selection of cheeses and preserved meats, fruit of the unlimited curiosity of Angelo Bissolotti one of the proprietors of this singular Milanese meeting place. Particularly rich in salumi, the Osteria offers the cured ham of Sauris, mocetta from the Val D'Aosta, sopressa from Brarda and ciauscolo from the Marches and Umbria. Equally unforgettable are the smoked Sardinian eels, the goat cheese or eggplant tortelli in thyme sauce, the gnocchi with duck ragù or the vegetable pappardelle in taleggio cream. Jolando De Colo's rolled goose breast was the inspiration for their much-requested lasagnette with leeks.

DUCK SPECK

ROYAL AGARICS ENHANCE THE DELICATE FLAVOR OF DUCK SPECK

Duck Speck is one of the most well known products in Jolanda De Colo's lineup. On its own it makes for an elegant antipasto. The smoking process, which employs a mixture of aromas derived from burning beech wood, juniper berries and cloves, determines its characteristic flavor. At Da Toni they add a personal touch to further enhance this delicacy: paper thin slices of the duck speck garnished with tender watercress sprouts and raw royal agarics (amanita caesaria, the preferred mushroom of the Caesars) are dressed with a drizzle of the finest quality extra virgin olive oil and served with buttered crostini aromatized with a few drops of balsamic vinegar. Best accompaniment: a young, but well structured white wine such as a Tokaji Friulano.

ERNEST HEMINGWAY, AN EXCEPTIONAL GUEST

Gastronomy and art, culture and tradition: there is a place for all of them at Da Toni in Gradiscutta di Varmo (Udine). The Morassutti family began its commitment to the restaurant business in 1929. Chino Ermacora, Friuli's great proponent was among the first to discover this *buen retiro* and he was soon followed by Ernest Hemingway, Amedeo Giacomini, Elio Bartolini and many others. The guiding principle, today sustained with great professionalism and style by Aldo Morassutti and his wife Lidia, is that of offering an updated regional cuisine, which includes dishes derived from age-old recipes presented with respect to modern canons of proportion and elegance. This well considered cuisine is matched by a rich cellar. The wine list includes the finest Italian crus and nearly all of the top producers in Friuli Venezia Giulia. Nor should the house wines (Camarin) be overlooked. Aldo Morassuti personally selects these reds and whites from all of the region's DOC zones. Da Toni's chef, Roberto Cozzarello, has made a name for himself as a standard bearer of quality cuisine.

TRADITIONAL GOOSE SALAMI

JEWISH TRADITION AND GRANDMOTHER SARA'S SALAMI

Legend has it that the Doge's personal secretary purchased traditional goose salami only from Righetto, who traded from a store in the shadow of St. Mark's bell tower. His product was famous for the consistency of its quality. Grandmother Sara's salami (as it was then called) was made from goose meat and was the only one that could claim kosher status. Its origins merge with that of the Venetian ghetto in the mid fifteenth century. Many documents from the period attest to the production and sale of this singular product in the ghetto. Antonello Pessot began his search for the recipe over twenty years ago, eventually learning it directly from the last traditional Jewish butcher in Venice, Luciano Curiel. The production technique Jolanda De Colo uses today is the same one imparted by Curiel. The flesh of the goose's neck is hand sewn to provide a casing that is subsequently filled with lean goose meat (knife-cut to a medium dice), seasoned with salt, pepper, and pimento. The salami are then stitched closed and allowed to mature.

AN ANTIQUE RECIPE FROM THE VENETIAN GHETTO

Traditional goose salami, a true delicacy with a long and illustrious history, is of Jewish origin. Its creation can be traced to the fifteenth century since the first official documents that testify to the existence of this extraordinary product of Venetian Jewish tradition date from that time.

Over the centuries, kosher butchers passed the recipe down through oral tradition, much like a secret formula. Panisson is one of the few remaining Venetian delicatessens to offer traditional goose salami, prepared according to the early recipe traceable to the ghetto.

GOOSE SALAMI FROM FRIULI

GOOSE: AN IDEAL COMPLEMENT TO PORK

At one time in Friuli it was common for poor farmers to use goose meat to compensate for the inferior quality of their pork. A pig was a notable investment given the expense related to keeping such a voracious animal well fed. The goose, on the other hand could procure its own food independently. Thus it became a fixture in the barnyard of the modest farmer and was a great help to his family in making ends meet. Their cured pork products, most particularly their salamis, benefited from the addition of goose meat. Necessity lay at the root of a tradition that is continued to this day in Friuli: a mixture of the two types of meat in salami. The characteristic flavor may be easily distinguished from that of whole pork salami because it is sweeter, more delicate and also less fatty.

SPECK – WHERE SINGLES ARE AT HOME

The unusual thing about the Prennushi family delicatessen is not is location on Trieste's only street closed to automobile traffic, but its decision to cater to a very specific clientele. The dynamic Prennushi siblings Katrin, Rrak and Zef made the conscious decision to tailor their offerings to young consumers who want to eat well, but who may also have problems of space. Every item offered at Speck is made to measure in mono-portions. The perfect destination for the urban single, here quality does not depend on quantity and all sorts of specialties, from French cheeses to the best salumi, are on hand. Jolanda De Colo supplies this unique delicatessen with a local standard, the traditional goose salami, rediscovered by Antonello Pessot – in single-serving portions – of course.

Goose Prosciutto Cotto

A Light Balanced Diet

A healthy, balanced diet necessarily takes into consideration the nutritional qualities of each single component. The common belief that lighter, less caloric foods are tasteless and without nutritional merit is not always correct. There are many foods that offer both low fat content and great satisfaction, even for the most refined palate - prosciutto made from cooked goose being fine example. At Jolanda De Colo careful, artisanal production assures a product with a fine, delicate flavor and a calorie count which should satisfy even the most health-conscious. The goose's ultimate success, however, is bound to the place of honor it has always assumed in traditional cuisine where it often appears as the protagonist of holiday dinners.

Collector's Flavors in the Heart of Florence

Florentine gastronomes know where to find the finest selection of high-quality foodstuffs. At the Macelleria Azzari where tradition reigns, the father and son team of Paolo and Adriano have put together a veritable collection of delicacies. They personally select the high quality, typically Tuscan products offered in addition to domestic and imported wines, French and Spanish cheeses, Tuscan and Sicilian olive oils. The real finds however are to be had among the many artisanal Tuscan salumi and prosciutti, produced according to age-old traditions. The Azzari's also hold the Florentine exclusive on the bread of Lionel Poîlaine, which arrives daily from Paris, and, of course, Jolanda De Colo's products make a fine showing.

GOOSE PROSCIUTTINO CRUDO

SALAMI WITH A SIX HUNDRED YEAR HISTORY

The domestication of the goose dates back to the neolithic period when, it is believed, man first relegated to captivity the descendants of the wild gray goose. Given the notable history of this symbiosis, it is hardly surprising that the first prosciutto crudo made from goose meat can be traced back several centuries. In Friuli Venezia Giulia this minute salami was produced in San Daniele as early as 1400.

Presenting the same form as the common prosciutto derived from pork, prosciuttino crudo d'oca is much smaller in size. In fact, its weight seldom exceeds 300 grams (10.5 ounces). Both are produced in the same manner, but the goose-based product differs in the length of its salting, drying and maturation phases, which are much shorter.

THE HEIGHT OF TASTE IN THE CENTER OF FASHION

Since Milan's Via Montenapoleone has become the epicenter of Italy's fashion industry, the simple food emporia that serve the district have also changed their look and its salumeria can credibly market themselves as a cult destination of haute gastronomy. Located in an internal courtyard, La Corte di Montenapoleone offers the best to a truly exclusive clientele. Given its location, it has become the neighborhood stop for many of the city's top names in the fashion industry and the international figures that revolve around the trade. Inevitably, a portion of La Corte has evolved into an open-air restaurant that offers recherché dishes made from the top quality ingredients which line its shelves.

PORCALOCA

THE FINEST MEAT FOR PROSCIUTTO WITH CLASS

The goose offers interesting possibilities as a counterpoint to other flavors. Porcaloca, a salume that owes its creation to the unstinting curiosity of Antonello Pessot, provides one of the finest examples of this notion. This singular salume utilizes an entire boned goose. Its flesh is evenly spread out to serve as a wrapper for a filling of lean goose and pork. The outer layer, called the *paletot*, is then hand stitched to complete the closure. Each bundle, (bound to give it a uniform shape), is baked for over ten hours and then lightly smoked. The particular characteristics of the goose fat lend this baked ham an unmistakable flavor, which is similar to that of Prague ham, though more intense. Porcaloca is ideally served thinly sliced, but it may also be roughly cut and lightly sautéed. In this case it is best served hot with mashed potatoes and sauerkraut.

AN ARRAY OF THE FRESHEST DELICACIES

Deciding to indulge in the Friday lunch at Enzo Roncati's delicatessen means letting yourself in for an array of dishes made from the freshest fish. Fresh, honest flavors have always distinguished the offerings of his three chefs who continually revise their menu following the course of the seasons. Game, handmade pasta, typical local salumi and cheeses as well as specialty foods chosen from all over Italy and wines which are personally selected by Mr. Roncati are just a fraction of the offering of this exceptional deli which has made quality and courtesy its watchwords since 1948.

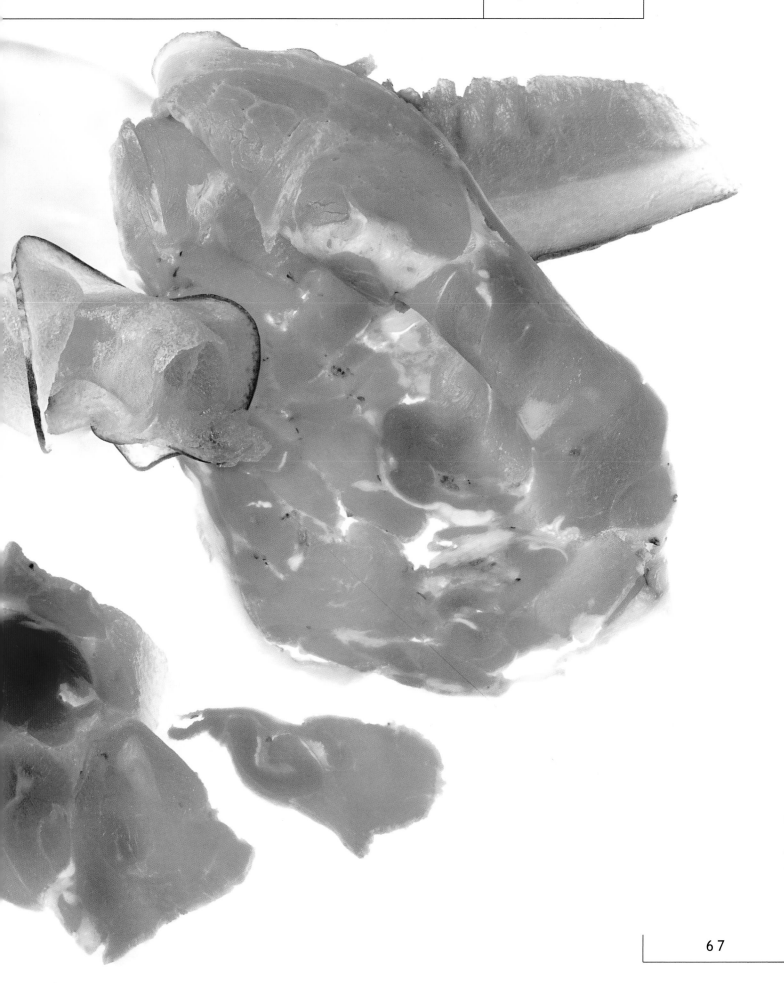

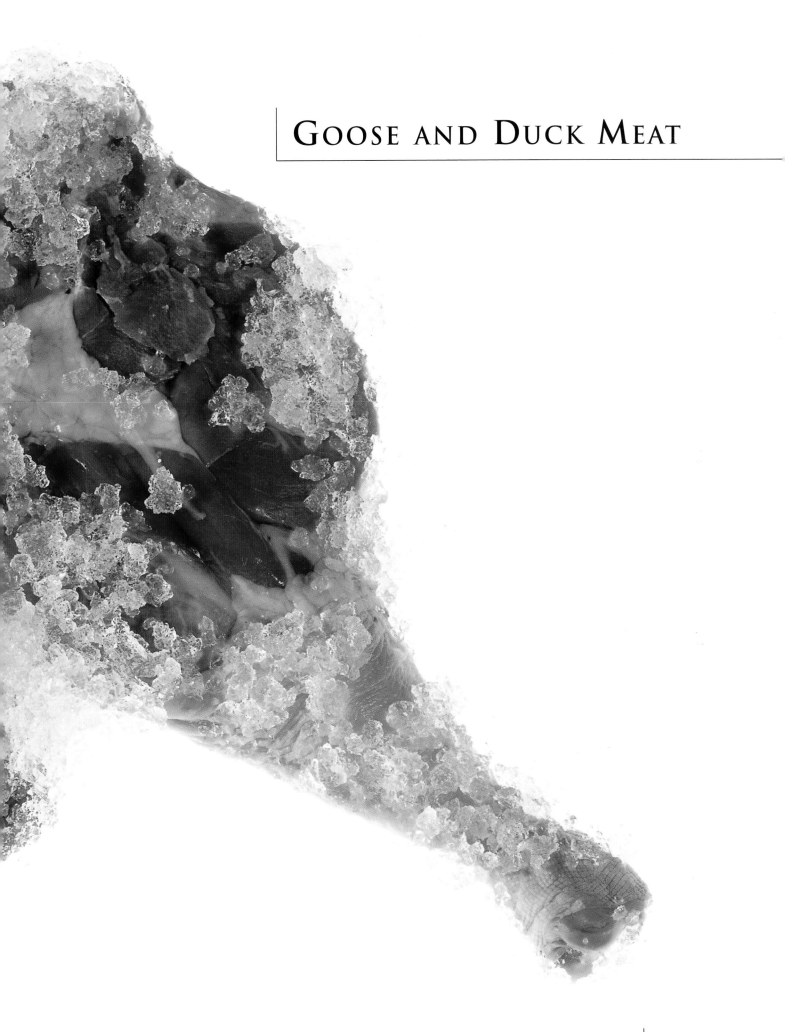

Duck Legs

The Rosy, Delicate, Flavorful Meat of the Moulard Duck

Often goose and duck are proposed in such a generic fashion that diners risk confusing them. Yet the flesh of each of these fowl has a distinct personality that makes it particularly suited to different uses. Moreover, the various breeds present further distinctions, with each type of duck or goose being better adapted to one type of preparation as opposed to another. For its duck confit Jolanda De Colo uses only the Moulard duck (also chosen for foie gras production) whose meat is particularly well suited to this use. Its light, rosy colored flesh is quite tender. When preparing a whole roast duck, the Barberie duck is an excellent choice.

French Ambiance for Refined Palates

At Miramonti L'Altro the atmosphere is elegant and cordial. Situated in a neoclassic villa, the restaurant's gray and white dining room offers two large bow windows that overlook a small garden. Its carefully planned menu offers selections based on traditional local cuisine enriched by the French touch of chef Philippe Léveillé whose gallic sensibility is particularly evident in dishes containing lamb, kid, duck and guinea hen. His multi-course tasting menu offers an opportunity to sample a series of dishes (in addition to an excellent selection of cheeses and pastries) in just the right succession. Over 1,200 labels appear on Miramonti L'Altro's wine list, which includes an ample selection of Italian and French wines as well as those from the emerging wine-producing nations.

GOOSE LEGS

COMPACT, TENDER, FLAVORFUL MEAT

Goose legs have been described as delicate, tender, succulent morsels. One of haute cuisine's richest resources, they lend themselves to many different preparations from the refined to the simple. In any case, it is their particular flavor that makes the difference. Jolanda De Colo is especially attentive to the selection process, choosing only the finest examples from its farms to be presented in this cut, so well adapted to single serving portions. The Toulouse and Emden breeds are most suitable since the compact nature of their flesh assures that flavor and tenderness will not be sacrificed during the cooking process. Jolanda De Colo's allowing the geese to range freely, nourishing themselves on grass and corn further guarantees excellent results.

THE SECRET PASSAGES OF FLAVOR

Arranging to dine at Da Gigetto is relatively simple. Gaining access to its owner's inner sanctum is a bit more difficult. A steep staircase and a subterranean passage lead to this special cellar which is one of the most intriguing to be found in the Italian restaurant world. It is the brainchild of Luigi Bortolini the warm and energetic owner of Da Gigetto, whose many dining rooms and secret chamber are by now legendary. Here the cuisine is simple, drawing its inspiration from local products and traditions. The hills around Treviso are famous for dishes based on slow grilling on a rotisserie. Goose legs are a classic preparation and though the recipe is deceptively simple the resulting flavor is one of a kind, truly singular.

WHOLE ROAST GOOSE

AN EXTRAORDINARILY INTENSE DISH

How many times have we heard that not a single part of a goose ever goes to waste? Like the pig it can be used in many different ways, a great advantage to rural domestic economy. In one sense however, the goose beats its historic rival: it can be served whole, presented in all its glory to appreciative guests. An extraordinarily intense dish, a whole roast goose offers great culinary possibilities. Its flesh offers a wide range of flavors and textures from the delicate breast meat to the more flavorful dark meat. Even the less noble parts contribute exquisite gustatory sensations.

GERMANO AND BERTILLA – ITALY'S EXPERTS ON THE GOOSE

Italy's authority on geese is surely Germano Pontoni: chef, researcher and author of two books on the subject. A great promoter of the *palimpede*, he cites the quality of its meat, the affection it inspires and the possibility of using all of its parts to great advantage as the goose's top selling points. If the culinary merits of this bird have, to a large extent, been rediscovered in Friuli Venezia Giulia it is due to his tireless, even loving, promotion. With his wife "Mamma" Bertilla he has rediscovered many traditional recipes that employ the goose, but these studies have perhaps found their finest expression in his recipe for whole roast goose.

BONED GOOSE LEGS

A VERY SPICY GOOSE

The spices employed (a house secret) lend fresh meats a completely different texture and flavor, especially the tender breasts and firm thighs of the geese which are used in one of Del Doge's most requested recipes. The finest cuts are allowed to marinate for 24 hours in a mixture of white wine and the spice blend. In the succeeding phase it's the chef's touch that makes the difference. He must hand cut the meat into uniform cubes that are then slowly braised. Chopped goose liver plays an important role in flavoring the braising liquid that is similarly spiced. Lovely and refined the resulting dish is best served with a well-structured wine such as a Merlot del Collio – direct and intense with traces of blackberries and other woodland fruits.

THE DOGE'S VILLA

Situated in a world-class location, the Del Doge Restaurant in Passariano di Codroipo occupies the west wing of (the Palladian?) Villa Manin, which dates from the 18th century. This final residence of the Venetian doge has been transformed into a restaurant complex with alla carte service for seventy occupying a portion while the larger spaces are given over to various banquet halls which can accommodate up to five hundred diners. Mario and Delino Macor, whose professional skills were refined at Rome's Excelsior and Grand Hotels, look after the dining rooms and cellar while their brother Severino commands the kitchen. Their tenure at Del Doge, which began in 1973, has been marked by a number of prizes and citations. In fact it was with this recipe for Manin Goose with Polenta that they won First Place in the Fogher D'Oro competition at Valeggio sul Mincio in 1979. Their excellent cellar, managed by Delino exhibits a predilection for Friuli's many fine wineries.

FRESH GOOSE BREAST

THE PRIDE OF THE GOOSE IS ITS BREAST

The goose has played anything but a secondary role in the history of fine cuisine. Traditionally, it held a place of honor in the banquets of the nobility as is confirmed by a wide range of contemporary accounts. Cast into a sort of culinary oblivion due to the aggressive promotion of pork, it never quite succeeded in reconquering a primary position in our diets. Certainly the necessity of closely monitoring its cooking time is a bit alien to the "heat and eat" culture of the modern, harried housewife. Yet, a fresh goose breast is a very versatile cut. offering singular flavor, open to a number of possible cooking techniques and capable of surprising and imaginative pairings with other flavors. The secret to avoid drying its tender flesh is a careful balance between a high cooking temperature and direct exposure to heat.

CREMONA'S ARTISTS OF TERRITORIAL CUISINE

The Fagioli brothers are at the helm of a typical trattoria located in the Cremona hinterland. Finding it takes a bit of effort, as it is hidden away in Bolzone, a tiny suburb of Ripalta Cremasca, but once discovered Via Vai offers the finest local cuisine. A certain respect for culinary tradition reigns here and the goose is an undisputed protagonist. One of the house's classic dishes is *Cabbage Stuffed Breast of Goose*, a perfect offering for this celebration of Jolanda De Colo's products.

Stefano Fagioli and his wife animate Via Vai's dynamic kitchen and they are true artists when it comes to preparing goose pâté and a number of traditional salumi made from goose meat. Marco, the family wine expert and irrepressible communicator, looks after the dining room. Frequently visited by the Milanese when they're in their pastoral mode, Via Vai seems to hold a special place in the hearts of its top newspaper journalists.

FRESH DUCK BREAST

AN INTERNATIONAL DISH

Once a staple of classic cuisine, this dish was, for quite some time, inappropriately called fillet of duck. This malapropism can be traced to the restaurant world and not the home kitchen and is probably due to the physical characteristics of this particular cut. A duck breast presents firm, compact flesh with little residual moisture. It benefits from a brief cooking time at a high temperature to seal in what little water it possesses. The crust created by the high heat prevents dehydration and insures a tender breast. Jolanda De Colo suggests that home cooks look for Moulard or Barberie ducks for this use and that pay particular attention to the cooking time.

HAUTE CUISINE – ALWAYS IN SEASON IN MILAN

Sergio Mei is responsible for the kitchen of one of Milan's most prestigious hotels, the Four Seasons. He brings to this position a considerable background in the hotel industry and years of study. The kitchen of a luxury hotel must be able to respond to the often-antithetical claims of quantity and quality as it must cover restaurant, banqueting and room services. Sergio Mei has built his reputation on the eclecticism and quality control that such a role demands. The author of a popular vegetarian cookbook and a docent at the Etoile school for professional chefs he has inspired and instructed many young chefs. Prior to assuming his post at the Four Seasons, chef Mei directed the cooking staff of the entire CIGA hotel chain.

BREAST OF CANETTE

CANETTE, THE FEMALE DUCK WITH THE ROSY FLESH

Breeders' classifications of ducks are not limited to a division of the most suitable strains for meat, livers or feathers. A further subdivision is made according to sex, a characteristic that presents different possibilities, particularly with regard those breeds destined for cooking. This is particularly true of the Barberie duck. The young female specimen, harvested when at most 60 days old, is called a canette, and is much valued for its delicate flesh and thin, lean skin. Its small stature also contributes to its suitability to haute cuisine as its tiny breast provides a perfect single serving portion. The Barberie may be distinguished by the color of its flesh with the males presenting dark, intensely colored meat and the canettes the characteristic delicately flavored, rosy colored flesh. A proper equilibrium between temperature and cooking time is essential for correctly prepared duck. Like all water fowl its meat tends to be rather dry. To avoid ruining the flavor, the right degree of moisture must be maintained. This requires a high flame distributed over a relatively short cooking time.

THE CUISINE OF TRIESTE – A MITTELEUROPEAN AFFAIR

Situated at a geographic and cultural crossroads, Trieste is the site of a singular fusion of all that is Eastern European and all that is Mediterranean. It is here that the Latin, Slavic and Germanic cultures achieve their most successful and original blend, as rich histories and humble stories of everyday lives flow together into the Adriatic.
Mario Suban attributes his love of the restaurant business, and the ease with which he confronts the area's distinctive cultural mix, to his mother who hailed from the Croation side of the Gulf of Trieste. Each year he hosts an exchange program between restaurants from Trieste and Hungary. The classic Mitteleuropean cuisine that is featured has two constants: the hearty cabbage-based soup known as jota and roasted veal shanks which are granted the place of honor.

Fresh Goose and Duck

Gustatory Counterpoint: The Sweet Goose and the Full Flavored Duck

From a taxonomic standpoint both geese and ducks belong to the family of the *antedate*. Yet, from a gastronomic point of view they present different characteristics. The goose offers a sweeter, more delicate flavor that can nevertheless reach notable levels of intensity in its "noble" portions such as the breast and the liver. Duck meat delivers a stronger, more substantial flavor with is liver (also quite good for foie gras) following suit. Jolanda De Colo offers a wide range of products derived from Toulouse and Emden geese as well as Moulard and Barberie ducks. In order to further assist the restaurant sector, which often requires single-serving portions, it has included the canette among its many offerings. This smaller, female Barberie duck presents tender, rosy flesh and great flavor.

The Long Season of a Delicate Flower

A gastronaut in search of fine cuisine in San Quirino need look no further than La Primula (The Primrose). Its chef Andrea Canton comes from a long line of restaurateurs and his personal achievement is the key to its success. The winner of a number of gastronomic competitions, he has become Friuli Venezia Giulia's most decorated chef. Yet, none of this pomp invades La Primula whose understated interior is home to warm and genuine hospitality. Even though the sea remains some distance away, its influence can often be detected in Andrea's cuisine (his branzino bottarga should not be missed). Chef Canton's strong tie to regional cuisine is reflected in his choice of recipe for Jolanda De Colo: Duck Tortelli.

SPECIALTY MEATS

SMOKED VENISON

A REVIVAL OF THE SUMPTUOUS FLAVORS OF THE COURT

In the past venison was often served at the high point of royal banquets, its various cuts sometimes recomposed so that nearly the entire animal might be suggested in a fantastic presentation emblematic of the pomp and luxury of the court. In Europe changing dietary habits have caused venison to be eclipsed by other types of game. With the introduction of smoked venison , Jolanda De Colo has made a symbolic attempt to recoup the regal tradition long associated with this dish. Gentle smoking satisfies the modern palate, which prefers game whose essentially wild taste is somewhat downplayed, yet this technique remains within the scope of traditional methods of preserving this specialty meat.

ALPINE TRADITION IN THE SHADOW OF MILAN'S CATHEDRAL

A small corner of the Trentino survives in the center of Milan where diners can enjoy the hearty flavors of mountain cuisine. Its many fine salumi make for a first class antipasto, but the essence of this cuisine, so firmly tied to the land, is best expressed in its many hearty soups. This authentic mountain retreat, so unusual amid the bustle of the city, offers both meat and fish and a rich dessert selection as dictated by tradition. For Jolanda De Colo, it developed a simple and inviting dish based on smoked venison.

PITÌNA

A Shepherds' Intuition for Refined Tables

Pitìna is a type of preserved meat that has been produced for quite some time. It is believed to have been invented by the shepherds who grazed their flocks in the high pastures (Andreis, Claut, Montereale Valcellina) among the mountains surrounding Pordenone. Jolanda De Colo has refined the original strong flavor of pitìna and lent it a longer shelf life. Chef Andrea Bordignon has given this rustic product a rather interesting interpretation: Thin strips of pitìna are briefly sautéed and then deglazed with high quality vinegar. Arranged on a bed of rocket (or, when in season, Treviso endive) they are then topped with an ultra thin slice of "drunken" cheese. A speciality of the local dairy in Lavariano, this curious product is allowed to age submerged in grape pomace. A Tokaji Friulano makes the perfect accompaniment.

The Goose, Of Course, Served with Charm

The tiny, charming Trattoria Blasut ,affectionately known as Yum Yum, is furnished with 18th century Friulian antiques. Located in Lavariano (the Roman Laberius) it is run with great energy and style by Dante Bernardis, also the originator of a local festival celebrated in November on the Feast of Saint Martin which pairs the goose with each year's new wine. Andrea Bordignon, a veritable institution in the Friulian restaurant world presides over the kitchen. His cuisine draws its primary inspiration from the territory though it is equally attentive to that of colleagues who make good use of each season's bounty. The well-stocked cellar is Dante's territory. A great believer in maintaining a personal relationship with producers he counsels, "Never rely on the telephone." Friulian wines dominate, but his selection also includes a significant number of labels from the Piedmont, Tuscany, Campania and Sicily.

CURED BEEF

COLD SMOKED SIRLOIN

This American sirloin steak seemingly has little in common with smoked salmon, but it is actually cured in a similar manner. After a period of experimentation, Jolanda De Colo discovered just the right breed for this delicately cured product: Nebraska Herefords, allowed to graze freely all year round. The delicate taste of this tender meat is achieved through a careful curing process. After dry salting, the beef is cold smoked over burning beech wood. These combined techniques allow the meat to retain its fine texture without sacrificing flavor.

A PRINCELY RESIDENCE FOR REGAL BANQUETING

The Carafa princes' splendid home was purchased by the Confalone brothers of Andria with the idea of turning it into one of the finest restaurants in Puglia. The enormous palazzo, which had fallen into disrepair, was completely restored and transformed into one of the area's grandest facilities, capable of hosting three wedding banquets simultaneously. While large numbers of guests are entirely within Villa Carafa's range, quality is never sacrificed to quantity. The professional team which staffs the kitchen and dining rooms is perfectly capable of maintaining the rapid pace and fine service such surroundings demand. This imposing 17th century villa is surrounded by a beautifully landscaped park; rich in Mediterranean flora.

MARINATED BEEF CARPACCIO

FRESH ANGUS BEEF WITH A TOUCH OF SPICE

The Angus breed, which originated in Scotland, is notable for its large stature, a quality that is sometimes so pronounced that the females fail to produce enough milk for their calves. Perfectly adapted to the dry climate of the high fertile plains of Argentina, Angus cattle have done so well in South America that they have become the preferred breed. Jolanda De Colo selects the finest Angus beef for its marinated carpaccio. Despite its raw appearance, the meat is actually salted and spiced, a process that confers a fine flavor and a pleasing aroma. The carefully trimmed fillets are allowed to marinate for over three weeks in brine enriched with 21 different herbs and spices including coriander, bay leaf, mace and cinnamon.

A NOBLE RESIDENCE WHERE TRADITION REIGNS

In the heart of the Murgia an imposing eighteenth century villa, built on the sight of a Medieval fort, is now home to a multi-purpose facility for receptions, banquets and business meetings. Restored twenty years ago by the Pasculli family, the villa takes its name from the large square watchtower (originally called Torre Forte and subsequently Torre Quadra) that stands at the center of its grounds. The Counts Rogadeo, former inhabitants of the property were responsible for the construction of the chapel (16th century) and the stables (17th century). Now completely restored, these structures house a large banquet room, while the library and the granary were converted to two smaller meeting rooms. Giuliana Santagat Pasulli and her brother Domenico, the present day hosts of this imposing complex, propose a cuisine characterized by a successful blend of tradition and innovation. Jolanda De Colo's marinated beef carpaccio is served here with sautéed spinach redolent of butter.

SAN MARCO TENDERLOIN

PORK TENDERLOINS WITH CITRUS ZEST AND SAUCE

Jolanda De Colo produces a special pork tenderloin in San Marco, near Palmanova (UD). The curing and ageing processes employed set this unique product midway between prosciutto and carpaccio. It is precisely these entirely natural methods that give the meat its rosy color, pleasant aroma and tenderness - characteristics that make it a fine choice for an antipasto or cold entrée. The secret ingredient in this case is sugar, a powerful drying agent when it comes into contact with moist, raw meat.

Orange and lemon zest and a touch of salt exalt the singular flavor of this tenderloin. The cut is familiar to all of us, but the chef's touch immediately transforms this already unique product.

REGIONAL CUISINE WITH A LIGHT TOUCH

Verona is a city rich in history and Maffei, one of its finest restaurants, is hardly an exception. It occupies the noble palazzo erected over the sight where, twenty centuries earlier, the Romans dedicated their temple to Jupiter. Today, it might be called a temple of gastronomy thanks to the Angelo Ruatti whose attention to detail and quality have literally transformed the restaurant in as little as two years. Though only thirty-five years old, he can already boast twenty years experience in the kitchen having begun his apprenticeship in 1980 in his native city of Cles (TN). Ruatti's goal is to rediscover and revisit the territory's original cuisine, utilizing local, natural products. His cuisine is all about lightness and bringing out the best in ingredients without recourse to lengthy cooking times or heavy sauces.

COOKED SMOKED PORK JOWL

TENDER, BUT WITH A DECISIVE FLAVOR

Pork is a seemingly inexhaustible source of flavor presenting many variations from the strong and decisive to the tender and nuanced. Surprisingly, cooked smoked pork jowl is of the latter category. Its delicate flavor is unmistakable and incomparable. This salume is commonly made from a cut of meat taken from the throat and jowl of the pig, transversed by at least two significant veins of fat. Jolanda De Colo gently steams the meat then binds it to give it its characteristic form and finally smokes it lightly. Unlike the cured pork jowl, which is used in many Italian recipes, this smoked version may be served thinly sliced with a touch of salt and pepper.

FINE WINES AND WORLDLY DELIGHTS

Mauro Lorenzon's unusual decision, to open his wine bar from six in the evening until six the following morning, was made at the outset, as was his commitment to offering the best Italian and imported wines. His wine bar is, in fact, one of the very few places where one can order vintage wine by the glass at any time. Its raw bar, continually restocked with oysters and periwinkles, is a legitimate source of pride and has made Caneva synonymous with Venetian nightlife. The products of Jolanda De Colo could only be at home here.

Leg of Lamb

Lamb *Prosciutto*

Its tender, delicately flavored meat has made lamb a much sought after dish, but its adaptability to a wide range of recipes is the characteristic that has made it a favorite of chefs worldwide. Jolanda De Colo has made it possible for lamb-based specialties little known in Italy to acquire a following. Such is the case with its gigot or lamb *prosciutto*. Its distinctive flavor is attributable to the tender age of the animals selected. Their rich diet and limited movement guarantee light colored, nearly white flesh, barely tinged with rose. These gigots are first deboned, then salted, marinated and finally gently steamed along with thyme. The addition of this herb takes the edge off the flavor of the meat, making just a bit less sharp.

Original Offerings

Tracing the origin of the name Sosta del Rossellio is not a straightforward task. One needs to know a little art history and a little local history to solve the puzzle presented by this Florentine wine bar. The street on which it is located is named for the Antonio and Bernardo Rossellino, Tuscan sculptors of the second half of the fifteenth century. This same street was also the site of an inn (sosta) that once served the horse traffic heading towards Bologna. The modern wine bar, located not far from this original travelers' stop, offers today's clients a selection of over three hundred wines from all over the world, pasta based primi piatti, and secondi featuring lamb, duck and goose and finally a choice of over 160 different cheeses. The desserts are particularly interesting and may be savored on the veranda or at one of the tables near the fireplace. Don't miss the *Red pepper bavarian cream with mint sauce* or the *Blancmange with physalis and chocolate*.

SASAKA

WHIPPED LARD AND SMOKED BREAST OF GOOSE – A DELICACY

Sasaka, which is essentially whipped lard, was once a major source of sustenance for the poor miners and mountaineers who lived in the Iron Passage, the portion of Friuli that borders Austria and Slovenia. Jolanda De Colo's version is enriched with smoked breast of goose and has found quite a following among refined palates. To make this particular delicacy pork fat is finely chopped and then beaten to a dense, creamy, spreadable consistency. A cold weather dish, sasaka in its De Colo version can stand up to the most refined of antipasti.

PLEASANT CONVERSATION, DELICACIES AND... DISTINCTIVE GIFTS

Catullo may call to mind the classics, but in the case of this Cremona enoteca it's the proprietor's father who lent it his name. For over fifty years, this Catullo has offered its clientele an exclusive selection of enogastronomical products and friendly conversation. The eighteenth century furnishings of its two large rooms hold over three thousand different wines and spirits, one hundred cheeses (largely, but not solely, Italian and French), sweets and objects relating to food and wine. A client in search of an elegant gift might select a set of knives produced by Berti, Italy's oldest manufacturer (in Cremona a Catullo exclusive) or a liqueur dating from the 1800s, one of the many extraordinary bottles proudly preserved in its large cellar of over 1000 square meters. Whatever he selects, Catullo's client can count on express delivery worldwide.

THE KAISER'S HAM

HAPSBURG MEMORIES IN THE FLAVOR OF A SMOKED HAM

The history of Trieste is firmly linked to that of the Austro-Hungarian Empire. Its art, literature, language and customs clearly resound with an Austrian influence. Gastronomic tradition could hardly be exempt. A predilection for flavors appreciated on the other side of the Alps is particularly evident in the many uses of pork in the Triestine diet. The Kaiser's ham effectively symbolizes this Austrian influence. During the reign of Maria Theresa of Hapsburg, a salted, baked and smoked pork tenderloin known as *Kaiserfleisch* was widely consumed.

THE EMPEROR'S GARDEN

Visitors to Cormons can hardly help but note the Mitteleuropean influence that pervades everything from the city's architecture to the manners of its inhabitants. Even today it is not unusual to find portraits of the Emperor Franz Joseph in many places of business. For years the Zoppolati family has run the city's finest restaurant and here too a central European leitmotif can be detected. Giorgio Zoppolati, who oversees the dining room and the cellar, is particularly well versed in the wines of the Collio whose hills surround the city. The kitchen, under the able direction of his brother Paolo and their mother Maria has always given an important role to the meat course with *Kaiserfleisch* (also known as the Emperor's steak) being perhaps the most typically Mitteleuropean protagonist. Paolo has re-elaborated this dish for the modern palate just as he has reworked many traditional desserts, a talent which has made him a popular local television chef.

HONEY GLAZED TURKEY BREAST

A TYPICALLY ANGLO-SAXON SWEET AND SAVORY BLEND

The original recipe for honey glazed turkey breast has its roots in Anglo-Saxon cuisine where the contraposition of sweet and savory flavors is quite common. Simply prepared, this dish depends to a great extent on the quality of its ingredients. In Jolanda De Colo's version the finest turkey breasts are gently steamed and then vacuum-sealed with a glaze made from acacia-based honey. This final phase insures that the meat acquires its distinctive aromatic quality.

SAVING ENDANGERED DELICACIES

Claudio and Emilio Volpetti have made a mission of saving gastronomic specialties in danger of disappearing. Located in the heart of Rome's Testaccio district, for thirty years their delicatessen has not only supplied discerning customers, but has also acted as a neighborhood meeting place, a haven of old world courtesy in the bustling modern city. As early as 1900, the building that houses Volpetti served as a distribution center for the production of the shepherds from the surrounding countryside. Today it offers the salumi, cheeses, olive oils, wine, bread, caviar and truffles personally selected by its proprietors for their international clientele. This simple, welcoming bottega of the brimming shelves also offers take-out service and on-site tastings.

SALT AND FRESH WATER DELICACIES

Swordfish Carpaccio

From the Depths of the Mediterranean to Gourmet Tables

A solitary swimmer which prefers deep waters, the swordfish approaches the coast only in the Spring. Its firm delicately flavored flesh has a pinkish tone and is much appreciated not only for its nutritional value but also for the ease with which it may be prepared.

This easily recognized fish frequently achieves notable dimensions with some examples topping six hundred pounds Because of its large size, the swordfish is most commonly available in steaks taken from transverse sections - yet another factor which has contributed to its reputation as an easily prepared fish. For its swordfish carpaccio Jolanda De Colo selects only young Mediterranean specimens because age is an important factor in guaranteeing tenderness. With this product it has succeeded in uniting the modern predilection for raw fish with an antique method of conservation: dehydration through smoking.

Milan's Gastronomic Paradise

Dealing with lawyers every day is hardly a problem for Carlo Zoppi and Giuseppe Gallotti since the delicatessen that bears their names is just a few blocks from Milan's courthouse. Judges, attorneys, clerks and secretaries alike have all benefited from the helpful guidance of these two enterprising figures. In just under 300 square feet they have created a gastronomic paradise - a rich selection of prepared foods, sauces, cheeses, salumi and wines. While making a choice is not always easy when confronted with such abundance, once a selection is made the service is rapid and satisfaction is guaranteed. Carlo and Giuseppe are particularly proud of their Slim service. Blast chilling and vacuum packing techniques imported from France make it possible to preserve prepared foods whose cooking can be completed in the home kitchen in a matter of minutes – with absolutely no loss to nutritional value or flavor.

SALMON *INGOTS*

THE UNMISTAKABLE FLAVOR OF SALMON FROM THE HEBRIDES

Once a specialty of the British Isles, salmon has become an important element in the European diet and a regular feature on many tables even in the Mediterranean. The finest salmon, which come from the cold waters of the Hebrides, are selected by Jolanda De Colo for its ingots. Made from relatively small fish with intensely colored aromatic flesh, this particular cut (also known as the balik) is taken from the leanest portion of the dorsal fillet. Especially attentive to their preparation, Jolanda De Colo uses a light touch in the salting and smoking phases. This very natural treatment assures that the essential flavor of the salmon reaches the consumer.

ENOLOGY AND GASTRONOMY HAND-IN-HAND

Real passion knows no obstacle, not even that of family tradition. Despite the fact that he holds a law degree and his father is one of the most prominent attorneys of Gorizia, Luca Nanut could not resist the attractions of his first love, wine. He chose Trieste for his splendidly appointed wine bar where tasting reigns supreme. Here there is no obligation to order a whole bottle; excellent wines may be purchased by the glass.

Given his passion for wine, Luca could hardly renounce a similar excursus into the world of fine food. His wine bar offers a fine selection of salumi and preserved fish and, of course, there is no problem in finding just the right wine to accompany them. In Jolanda De Colo's salmon ingots Luca has found the perfect ingredient for his sashimi.

DILL MARINATED SALMON

WHEN APPEARANCE MAKES A DIFFERENCE

Gravlax is for many the classic preserved salmon. Traditionally, its production involves dry salting, but Jolanda De Colo's version prefers brine with the addition of spices and a generous portion of dill. (Wild fennel, chives and pink pepper berries also produce interesting results.) The Scottish salmon used in this case is not only marinated but also lightly smoked. Because relatively little salt is used the resulting product is more appropriately defined as fresh than preserved. While this gives it a short shelf life, it also accounts for its extraordinary flavor. Dill marinated salmon makes a lovely presentation. The green corolla, which surrounds each transverse slice, presents a marked contrast to the rosy hue of the salmon flesh. It may be served plain or with a touch of extra virgin olive oil.

A STRONGHOLD OF FLORENTINE GASTRONOMIC TRADITION

A rearing red lion clutching an olive branch has been the symbol of the Florentine guild of Oliandoli and Pizzicagnoli since the 1300s. The ten founders of the city's Convivium chose this familiar figure for its coat of arms because it so eloquently represents a link to the city's glorious gastronomic past. For over twenty years this organization has promoted rediscovery, study and preservation of traditional Florentine and Tuscan cuisine. A continuing commitment to these precepts lays behind the selection of cheese, salumi, fresh pasta, sweets and prepared foods which are offered daily to Convivium Firenze's clientele. A 14th century building, renovated in 1997 is the present home of this singular complex (called not so coincidentally, Canto del Paradiso) that includes individual tasting rooms and banquet halls.

BENBÈCULA SALMON

AROMATIC SMOKED SALMON

The cold uncontaminated waters of the Hebrides provide an ideal habitat for raising top quality salmon. This unique environment is home to the most highly prized specimens whose small size guarantees lean, flavorful, intensely colored flesh. Jolanda De Colo has long relied on these superior salmon furnished by Angus McMillan of Benbècula, a strong supporter of natural methods of fish farming.

Careful treatment of these excellent fish insures that their intrinsic qualities are preserved. The smoking process introduces an aromatic element, but the flavor of the final product is very much reminiscent of wild salmon. Jolanda De Colo's Benbècula salmon is available in sliced or unsliced sides or in the smaller balik cut.

A GASTRONOMIC BOUTIQUE IN THE HEART OF BARI

The historic center of Italy's cities is traditionally home to its oldest gastronomic emporia. Bari is no exception. Here Nicola Perini's Salumaio has long assumed the role of the classic stronghold of quality. Its thousands of products are among the best displayed (and described) in Italy. An astute businessman, Perini has recently opened a satellite shop in Bari's busy airport. There his son Giacinto gives travelers the chance to take home Puglia's finest burrata or the classic mozzarelle of Andria. Smoked fish is one of the Perinis' particular passions and they have always been attentive to their selection. Jolanda De Colo's Benbècula salmon was a natural choice for these consummate professionals.

Norwegian Salmon

From the North Sea to the Adriatic

It is a well known fact that salmon are great travelers, but their arrival on the shores of the Adriatic, in this case, at the Madonnina del Pescatore, requires a little human intervention. The services of a trusted importer are required. Over the years Antonello Pessot has repeatedly compared salmon from around the world (Scotland, Norway, Canada, Ireland, Nova Scotia, Alaska, Labrador and Terra Nova) in order to determine the many subtle variations in flavor which differing environments may present. The icy waters of the Norwegian fjords furnish a type of salmon that Jolanda de Colò treats with great care. A combination of woods is used in the traditional smoking process in order to exalt the flavor of this fish's firm, compact flesh. Norwegian salmon can be distinguished by its naturally light color and this seems a perfect complement to the product's refined, nearly sweet taste.

Noy Sushi, but Susci!

"My only doubt is whether to use chopsticks or a fork." Moreno Cedroni's ironic observation (from his best-selling book *Sushi & Susci*) reveals many things, his open, imaginative personality, but also his reflective, studious side. One of Italy's most talented and innovative young chefs, Cedroni has made sure that his personal take on sushi represented neither the exploitation of a trend nor mere imitation. His *susci* represents something more - a fusion of his experience in the kitchens of famous European chefs with Japanese technique and with his own personal gastronomic memory. (His childhood on the Adriatic offered many memorable dishes from the typical Adriatic fish soup to polenta with clams.)

With his wife Mariella, Cedroni has created one of the most esteemed restaurants in Italy, the Madonnina del Pescatore in Senigallia (AN). Here raw fish is only the point of departure for the Cedroni's exploration of the many possibilities offered by seafood. His continuous research has led him to combine fish and shellfish with rice, pasta, vegetables and even meat, or in this instance, with cheese. The results, which are often surprising are always right on the mark.

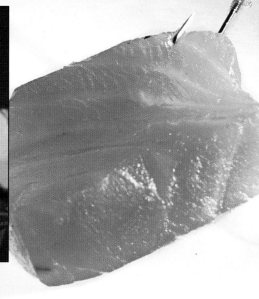

Iranian Caviar

Caviar Cappuccino?

Iranian caviar is one of Jolanda De Colo's best sellers and the key ingredient to Campiello's signature dish. A collaborative effort of its proprietor Dario Macorig and its chef Daniele Pocar, the recipe is based on a Russian classic. Served in a cup, this preparation features a base of creamy mashed potatoes topped by a layer of very cold whole-milk yogurt surmounted by the caviar garnished with a dusting of chives. A delicacy worthy of a Tsar, it is beautifully complemented by a well-structured Chardonnay with strong woody notes or, of course, a fine vodka. Russian tradition demands the latter and it makes for a heady combination, but one that certainly merits a try.

Where Champagne is the Favorite

Campiello in San Giovanni al Natisone (UD) is one of Friuli's finest restaurants. While its proprietor Dario Macorig can boast an apprenticeship in the Parisian temple of fine-dining the Tour d'Argent, his cuisine is more appropriately characterized as international than French. With his wife Maria he presides over the dining room and the restaurant's impressive cellar, though his own definition for this collection of thousands of bottles (where Champagne is the strong suit) is "monstrous." Chef Daniele Pocar commands the kitchen that can serve up to 120 guests. Campiello also offers nineteen guest rooms, which are often occupied by the German, Austrian and Swiss eno-tourists who make it their base for exploring the important DOC zones that are nearby.

IRANIAN CAVIAR

THERE IS CAVIAR AND CAVIAR

For caviar lovers the Caspian Sea represents paradise found since 95% of the world's caviar is harvested from the sturgeon who populate its waters. Both Russian and Iranian fishermen compete for these riches, but Jolanda De Colo is supplied solely by the latter for two important reasons. The first concerns hygiene. Iranian caviar is harvested, sorted, packaged and sold under state supervision and its processing plants conform to the European Union's standards of hygiene and safety. The second reason concerns quality. The Caspian's deepest waters are on the Iranian side. Not only do they never freeze, but strong currents continually aerate them. The gravel deposits, which characterize the sea floor on the Iranian side, also make for clearer, more limpid waters – all in all an ideal habitat for healthy sturgeon.

The various types of sturgeon, Beluga, Sevruga e Osetra produce eggs of differing dimensions and the caviar harvested from these fish is known by the same names. The light gray opalescent eggs of the Beluga are the largest and most highly prized.

SOMETHING OLD, SOMETHING NEW...

After completing his basic culinary studies in his native Germany, Ernst Knam served important apprenticeships in the kitchens of some of the most important restaurants in England and Switzerland before creating a sensation in Milan as Gualtiero Marchesi's pastry chef in 1989. After three years with the master, he chose independence, opening his own pastry shop, L'Antica Arte del Dolce in 1992. This new entrepreneurial role fit him so well l that he launched a second business, La Nuova Arte del Catering in 1996. Knam brought his passion, creativity and Teutonic rigor to the rapidly evolving catering sector and success was immediate. His crack staff and high- tech kitchen can handle events with up to 2000 guests without a single compromise in quality. Knam's continually evolving cuisine brilliantly balances tradition and innovation

MARINATED COD

A HISPANO-PORTUGUESE SPECIALTY

The Vikings are believed to have initiated the Scandinavian tradition of preserving cod. Its firm textured flesh, tempered by the icy waters of the North, easily lends itself to a number of conservation techniques. Through the centuries periods of great interest in the possibilities of this fish have alternated with others of near complete oblivion. At present it is enjoying a great revival with many restaurateurs reproposing traditional dishes which employ preserved cod in its two principal versions: stoccafisso and baccalà. Bacalao marinato represents just such a popular dish. Its roots are in the past but its flavor is particularly agreeable to the modern palate. Jolanda De Colo's version, which uses the finest cod, takes its inspiration from Hispanic and Portuguese traditional methods of drying and marinating this fish.

FINE FOOD AND HISTORY MEET IN UMBRIA

A palpable sense of history and tradition contribute to the singular atmosphere of the Locanda-Enoteca Onofri, an enogasronomical refuge nestled in the green hills of Umbria. Housed in an olive mill dating from the twelfth century, it looks out on the central piazza of the tiny town of Bevagna, just a few kilometers from Foligno. Visitors can hardly help but be attracted to this warm and inviting retreat. Its vaulted ceiling, rough hewn wooden floors, and large fireplace provide the perfect setting for a generous selection of salumi, cheeses, honey, jams and home-made pasta. Its impressive wine list features over seven hundred Italian and international labels, offering a wide range of combinations with the regional and creative cuisine of chef Mirco Nocchetti. Those wishing to prolong their stay may take advantage of one of the thirteen comfortable apartments that have been created in two adjacent medieval buildings.

WILD BELUGA STURGEON

THE FINEST SMOKED STURGEON FROM THE IRANIAN SHORES OF THE CASPIAN SEA

Smoked sturgeon is one of Jolanda De Colo's most successful niche products. Beluga (also known as uso uso) is the most prized variety of this fish with some specimens achieving particularly notable dimensions (up to thirteen feet in length and several hundred pounds). Captured during their annual migration from the Caspian Sea to the fresh waters of the rivers that feed it, they are characterized by a white, delicately flavored flesh whose particularly tender, flaky texture is produced by a gelatinous marbling. Chef Emanuele Scarello exalts these qualities in his Tartare of Smoked Sturgeon with Ginger Vinaigrette and Iranian Caviar, adding a piquant touch with pink peppercorns, chives and a spritz of white grape juice. A well-structured white wine such as a barrique aged Chardonnay makes the perfect accompaniment.

WINNING TECHNIQUES

The consensus is unanimous with clients waxing enthusiastic and the guides (Michelin, Espresso, Veronelli, Gambero Rosso, Gualt & Millau) heaping praise on the Trattoria degli Amici in Godia, a suburb of Udine. This particular success story has been ten years in the making with each of the four members of the Scarello family playing an important part. Recent induction into the organization Jeunes Restaurateurs d'Europe, has further confirmed the restaurant's reputation for innovation. Particularly attentive to cooking techniques, Chef Emanuele Scarello seeks to exalt the flavors of his top quality ingredients from local organic potatoes to hand-milled grains to herb-infused olive oils. He also offers a cheese selection that surpasses description. His fine food and excellent wine selection are warmly offered to a maximum of forty guests who may be accommodated in two small dining rooms.

THE RECIPES

THIRTY-ONE GREAT
INTERPRETATIONS

QUAIL WITH FOIE GRAS AND WILD HERBS

Vinicio Dovier

Ingredients for 4 servings:
4 quail, 200 g (7 oz) ground pheasant breast, 50 g (1 3/4) oz goose foie gras, 2 eggs, few sprigs of silene and dandelion greens, a pinch of poppy seeds, wild asparagus, salt and pepper

Preparation:
Bone the quail. Mix the chopped herbs and asparagus with the ground pheasant breast. Blend in the two egg yolks and season with salt and pepper. Divide the stuffing into four equal portions and place a piece of foie gras in the center of each. Fill the cavity of each quail. Arrange the birds on a double layer of aluminum foil (taking care to create a border to contain any escaping juices) and bake at 170° C (340° F) for 30 minutes. Serve on a bed of soft polenta and drizzle with the cooking juices.

DUCK FOIE GRAS WITH ALMONDS

Slavko Adamlje

Ingredients for 8-10 servings:
800 g (28 oz) goose foie gras, 100 g (3 1/2 oz) almonds, 40 g (1 1/2 oz) butter, 1 dl (scant 1/2 cup) cream, 1 dl (scant 1/2 cup) orange juice, zest of 1/2 an orange julienned, 1 leek, salt and pepper

Cut the foie gras lobes into 1.5 cm (1/2 inch) slices. Salt and pepper them and quickly sauté them in the melted butter. Add the almonds, the orange zest and deglaze with the orange juice. Midway through the cooking time, add the cream and mix well. Complete cooking and garnish with very finely sliced leeks.

WHITEFISH WITH FOIE GRAS

Riccardo De Prà

Ingredients for 4 servings:
1 whitefish (approx. 1 kg / 2 1/4 lbs), 12 small potatoes, 100 g (3 1/2 oz) goose foie gras, thyme, salt

Whitefish: Clean and scale the fish; remove the head (reserve) and tail. Rinse well. Fillet the fish and divide each fillet in half in order to obtain four portions. Eliminate any discolored flesh and all visible bones. Score the skin diagonally to enable the fish's natural oils to escape during cooking. Thread the fillets on skewers and grill them skin side down over very hot coals. They should cook through without turning.

Sauce: Cut the fish head in half and eliminate all traces of blood. Briefly simmer it with the backbone to remove any impurities. Transfer the solids to another pan, cover with water, add the thyme and gently simmer for 20 minutes, skimming as necessary. Peel and wash the potatoes and cook them in the fish broth. The starch they give off should thicken the liquid. Drain, reserving the broth and keep both the potatoes and the broth warm.
Cut the foie gras into thin strips, spread them on a plate and salt them lightly. Briefly cook the strips in the reserved, thickened fish broth. Arrange a portion of the grilled fish and the potatoes on each plate. Distribute a few strips of foie gras and nap with the sauce. Drizzle the fish with extra virgin olive oil and serve immediately.

SMOKED FOIE GRAS SPIRALS

Anna Tuti

Ingredients for 4 servings:
4 medium potatoes, 280 g (approx. 10 oz) smoked goose foie gras, 1 tablespoon butter, 75 ml (3 oz) milk, salt

Cook the potatoes for 30 minutes in boiling salted water. Mash them, incorporating the butter, salt and milk. Place a quenelle of mashed potatoes in the center of each plate, top with the foie gras spirals (obtained by using a truffle slicer or similar blade). Serve immediately.

TERRINE OF FOIE GRAS WITH BLACK TRUFFLES

Alessandro Scian

Ingredients for 6-8 servings:
400 g (14 oz) goose foie gras, 100 g (3 1/2 oz) black truffles, generous pinch of blended ground spices (cinnamon, cloves, cane sugar), 75 ml (3 oz) Port, 75 ml (3 oz) Calvados, salt and pepper

Gently open the lobes of foie gras and devein them. Place the foie gras in a non-reactive baking dish and dust with salt, pepper and the spice blend. Add the Port and Calvados; allow it to marinate for approximately 10 minutes. Remove the foie gras from the marinade and arrange it on a clean work surface. Position the truffle in the middle and close the foie gras around it. Transfer to a terrine and press to eliminate air pockets. Cover with plastic wrap and refrigerate for at least 4 hours. Remove the terrine from the refrigerator, transfer it to a blast chilling bag and cook in 70° C (158° F) oven on the steam setting for 30 minutes. Blast chill to cool quickly and unmold.
Place a slice of the terrine in the center of each plate. Serve with apple-grapefruit marmalade and slices of toasted pan brioche.

STUFFED BREAST OF GOOSE ON TOAST

Liano Petrozzi e Ida Tondolo

Ingredients for 4 servings:
200 g (7 oz) goose breast stuffed with foie gras, 1 small bunch of white grapes, 24 slices of pan brioche, a few drops of traditional balsamic vinegar of Modena, white wine such as Verduzzo, grape leaves

Cut the slices of pan brioche into decorative shapes and lightly toast them. Wash the grapes and cook them in a mixture of 2 parts Verduzzo to 1 part water, taking care that their skins to not split. Line a serving dish with the grape leaves. Arrange thin slices of the stuffed goose breast over the leaves; decorate with the toasts and the grapes. Sprinkle with a few drops of balsamic vinegar and serve. Should you prefer not to use the vinegar, top with a few butter curls.

TOC' IN BRAIDE

Daniele Cortiula

Ingredients for 4 servings:
Polenta: 200 g (7 oz) stone ground corn meal, 2 dl (scant 1 cup) water, 2 dl (scant 1 cup) milk, salt
Sauce: 300 g (10 1/2 oz) mixed creamy cheeses such as fresh ricotta, goat cheese and farmer cheese, 1dl (scant 1/2 cup) milk
Topping: 100 g (3 1/2 oz) butter, 50 g (3 tablespoons) stone ground corn meal, 200 g (7 oz) foie gras in torchon

Polenta: Bring the water and the milk to a boil; add the salt. Pour in the corn meal in a thin stream while stirring continuously so as not to form lumps. Cook for 30 minutes, mixing frequently. The finished polenta should be soft, not stiff.
Sauce: Melt the cheeses with the milk over a double boiler. Whip with an immersion blender to achieve a mixture with a creamy consistency.
Topping: Melt the butter in a small sauté pan and add the corn meal. Sauté until it turns a golden brown. This is called the "morchia."
Assembly: Place a portion of polenta on each plate; top with a generous helping of the cheese sauce and finish with a touch of the "morchia" and a few curls of foie gras. Serve immediately.

SCALLOPS OF FOIE GRAS WITH FOIE GRAS ICE CREAM

Daniela Gaddo Vedaldi

Ingredients for 4 servings:
360 g (12 1/2 oz) foie gras divided into 4 slices, 4 eggs, 2 tablespoons white vinegar, 60 ml (2 oz) heavy cream, 30 g (1 oz) traditional balsamic vinegar of Modena, 30 g (1 oz) smoked foie gras, salt and pepper, 60 g (2 oz) fig and nut bread, 100 g (3 1/2 oz) ice cream made with smoked foie gras

Bring water to a boil in a medium saucepan along with the white vinegar and a pinch of salt. Poach the eggs for 3 minutes with the aid of perforated egg poacher cups, remove the eggs and allow them to drain on paper towels. Briefly sauté the slices of foie gras in a non-stick pan, turning them once.
Place a slice of foie gras on each plate and top with a poached egg. Glaze with a sauce made from melting the smoked foie gras in the heavy cream with the addition of a little salt and pepper. Garnish with a few drops of the balsamic vinegar and a portion of the fig and nut bread topped with a spiral of smoked foie gras. Serve with a quenelle of ice cream made with smoked foie gras.

LASAGNA WITH LEEKS AND GOOSE BREAST

Paolo, Anna e Angelo Bissolotti

Ingredients for 4 servings:
200 g (7 oz) egg pasta such as lasagnette, 3 leeks, 1/2 liter (approx. 2 cups) béchamel sauce; 50 g rolled smoked goose breast, chives, grated Parmigiano Reggiano cheese, extra virgin olive oil, basil, salt and pepper

Cut the smoked goose breast into small pieces and sauté it in a little extra virgin olive oil, add the leeks (white portion only, sliced in rings) and allow the mixture to absorb all of the oil. Add the béchamel, mix well and add the chopped herbs. Cook the pasta until not quite done and drain on kitchen towels. Butter a baking dish and line it with alternating layers of pasta and the béchamel mixture until all have been used. Finish with a layer of béchamel; dust with the grated Parmigiano Reggiano cheese and bake in a 180° C (350° F) oven for approximately 15 minutes or until heated through and well browned on top.

DUCK SPECK WITH WATERCRESS AND ROYAL AGARICS

Roberto Cozzarolo

Ingredients for 4 servings:
240 g (8 1/2 oz) aged duck speck, 80 g (3 oz) watercress sprouts, 320 g (11 oz) royal agaric mushrooms*, parsley, Parmigiano Reggiano cheese, extra virgin olive oil, salt and pepper

Clean the mushrooms and slice them very thinly. Dust with chopped parsley and shards of Parmigiano Reggiano cheese. Drizzle with extra virgin olive oil; salt and pepper to taste and mix well. Place a portion of the mushroom and cheese mixture on each plate, top with thin slices of the duck speck, garnish with the watercress sprouts and drizzle with a little extra virgin olive oil.
*Due to its close resemblance to harmful varieties, this mushroom should be identified by a qualified authority before being eaten.

DUCK CONFIT WITH SICHUAN PEPPER

Philippe Léveillé

Ingredients for 4 servings:
4 duck legs, 10 cl (3 tablespoons) traditional balsamic vinegar of Modena, 1 teaspoon honey, 1/2 teaspoon sichuan pepper, 200 g (7 oz) butter, 5 shallots, 50 g (scant 1/4 cup) sugar, 20 cl (1 cup) heavy cream, 150 ml (2/3 cup) water, 1 kg (approx. 2 1/4 lbs) duck fat, salt and pepper

Salt and pepper the duck legs and sauté them in the butter for approximately 10 minutes or until well browned. Set the pan aside, reserving the fat. In a separate pan melt the duck fat, add the browned duck legs and cook them over a low flame for 4 hours. Eliminate all but a few tablespoons of fat from the reserved sauté pan and return it to the flame. Add the chopped shallots, sugar and honey; allow them to caramelize. Add the cream and water and continue cooking for 10 minutes. Add the sichuan pepper and salt to taste. Remove the duck legs from the fat and drain them well. Place them on a serving platter, nap with the sauce and garnish with seasonal vegetables.

MANIN GOOSE

Severino Macor

Ingredients for 4 servings:
1 goose thigh, 1 goose breast, 1 goose liver, 1/2 onion, 2 garlic cloves, 1 sprig rosemary, 150 ml (2/3 cup) dry white wine, 2 tablespoons extra virgin olive oil, zest of 1 lemon, salt and pepper to taste

Debone the goose (reserving a little of the fat) and cut the meat into small pieces. Transfer the meat to a non-reactive bowl and marinate it for 24 hours with the wine, 1 garlic clove and most of the rosemary. Dice the goose liver and sauté it in with the chopped onion in the reserved goose fat along with the olive oil. Drain the goose meat (reserving the marinade) and transfer it to the sauté pan with the liver and onions. Simmer over low heat for approximately 2 hours adding a little of the marinade from time to time. Finely chop the lemon zest along with a clove of garlic, and the remaining rosemary. Salt and pepper to taste and add a tablespoon of the mixture to the cooked goose. Serve with soft polenta.

GOOSE THIGHS

Ingredients for 4 servings:
4 goose thighs, 1/2 carrot, 1/2 onion, 1 celery stalk, rosemary, wild fennel, 1 bay leaf, extra virgin olive oil, dry white wine, salt and pepper.
For the zucchini: 2 zucchini, extra virgin olive oil, 100 g (3 1/2 oz) fine bread crumbs made from fresh bread, 50 g (scant 1/4 cup) grated Parmigiano Reggiano cheese, parsley, salt

Line an oiled baking sheet with the roughly chopped carrots, celery and onion. Salt and pepper the goose thighs and place them on top of the vegetables. Dust with the chopped herbs. Brown in a 180-190° C (350-375° F) oven, basting with dry white wine. Reduce the temperature to 120-130° C (250-270° F) and finish cooking. In the meantime, wash the zucchini and cut them into thin rounds. Blanch them in boiling salted water and cool immediately. On an oiled baking sheet, arrange overlapping slices of the zucchini to form four circles. Dust them with a mixture of the breadcrumbs, Parmigiano Reggiano, chopped parsley and salt and set them under the broiler until just browned. Place a goose thigh on each plate; accompany with a zucchini round, drizzled with the pan juices from the goose.

TRADITIONAL ROAST GOOSE

Ingredients for 6-8 servings:
1 goose (approx. 3 1/2 kilos or 7 3/4 lbs), zest of 1/2 a lemon, 1 Golden Delicious apple, 2 slices dry bread, 1 carrot, 1 celery stock, 1 onion, rosemary, 1 clove of garlic, dry white wine, 2-3 teaspoons wine vinegar, salt and pepper

Thoroughly wash the goose inside and out and dry it well. Salt and pepper it and fill the cavity with the halved apple and the bread. Truss the goose to maintain its shape. Place the goose in a Dutch oven and surround it with the roughly cut carrots, celery and onion. Add the garlic clove, a few sprigs of rosemary and just enough water to cover the bottom of the pan. Cover and roast in a 120-130° C (250-270° F) oven for 1 hour. Uncover, remove all visible fat floating on the pan juices and continue cooking until the goose is well browned. Baste from time to time with the wine, the vinegar and a little water (if necessary) so that the pan juices remain liquid. The aim is to brown the goose without drying it out. Test for doneness after approximately 3 hours by inserting a fork into the thigh. When the juices run clear, the goose is done. Remove from the oven and strain off the cooking juices, eliminating as much fat as possible. Carve the goose and transfer to a warm serving platter. Season the pan juices with a mixture made from blending finely chopped rosemary, a strip of lemon zest, a small amount of garlic and salt. Heat through and serve separately.

CABBAGE STUFFED BREAST OF GOOSE

Ingredients for 2 servings:
1 whole goose breast, 1/2 winter cabbage, 2 garlic cloves, 1 egg, 50 g (1 3/4 oz) grated Parmigiano Reggiano cheese, butter, nutmeg, sage, rosemary, dry white wine, salt and pepper

Make a lengthwise incision in the goose breast in order to create a pocket. Blanch the cabbage leaves in boiling salted water for 10 minutes. Drain and cool them immediately in cold water. Press out all of the excess water and chop the cabbage along with the garlic. Transfer to a large skillet and sauté in butter. Cool and add the grated Parmigiano Reggiano cheese, a pinch of nutmeg, the egg, salt and pepper. Blend well. Salt and pepper the goose breast; fill the pocket with the prepared stuffing and close the opening with a few stitches. Brown the breast in a sauté pan with a little butter, sage and rosemary. Deglaze with the white wine; salt and pepper to taste. Transfer the goose to an oiled baking pan and roast in a 200° C (390° F) oven for 20 minutes, basting with white wine midway through the cooking time. Remove from the oven and wrap the breast in aluminum foil. Allow it to rest for 5 minutes. Serve the sliced breast with polenta and nap with the cooking juices.

BREAST OF DUCK ROASTED IN A BEETROOT INFUSION

Ingredients for 4 servings:
2 duck breasts, approximately 300 g (10 1/2 oz) each, 1 cinnamon stick, 1star anise, 1 stalk lemongrass, 1 sprig wild fennel, salt
4 white asparagus spears, 4 green asparagus spears, 150 g (5 1/2 oz) chanterelle mushrooms, 4 small fennel bulbs, almond oil, 2 small artichokes, 8 cherry tomatoes, 4 baby turnips, 50 g (3 tablespoons) extra virgin olive oil.
Sauce: 200 g (7 oz) beet juice, pinch of hot red pepper, 10 g (1 tablespoon) honey, 150 g (5 1/2 oz) Gewürztraminer
Garnish: 12 fresh almonds, chopped chervil

Marinate the duck breasts in a mixture of the spices, almond oil and salt. Score the skin of the duck breasts and brown them in a sauté pan beginning with the incised side and then turning to evenly color both sides. Transfer to a 160° C (320° F) oven to complete cooking. (The internal temperature will register 46° C - 115° F). Slice the breasts diagonally and keep them warm.
Dilute the cooking juices with the Gewürztraminer and add the beet juice, honey and hot pepper. Reduce and filter.
Clean and trim the vegetables into evenly sized pieces (with the exception of the mushrooms and tomatoes); blanch them separately in boiling salted water. Sauté the vegetables in the extra virgin olive oil; add the mushrooms and tomatoes. Salt and pepper to taste and complete cooking.

Breast of Duck with Porcini Mushrooms
Mario Suban

Ingredients for 4 servings:
2 duck breasts, 3 garlic cloves, 1 onion, 1/2 liter (approx. 2 cups) Tokaji 3 Puttonyos, 2 porcini mushrooms, rosemary, thyme, 1 dl (scant 1/2 cup) veal stock, extra virgin olive oil, butter (not used)

Sauté the chopped onion and the herbs in a little extra virgin olive oil. Deglaze with the Tokaji and reduce by two thirds. Salt and pepper to taste; incorporate the veal stock; strain and reserve.

Score the skin side of the duck breasts and broil or roast them for 15 minutes at 180° C (350° F). Carefully clean the mushrooms; slice them thinly and sauté in extra virgin olive oil. Arrange alternating slices of duck and mushrooms on each plate; nap with the warm sauce and garnish with fresh herbs.

Duck Tortelli
Andrea Canton

Ingredients for 4 servings:
2-3 skinned duck thighs from which all fat has been removed, 2 onions, 2 shallots, 1 glass dry white wine, 2 tablespoons peeled, glazed San Marzano tomatoes, 1 tablespoon Parmigiano Reggiano cheese, 1 tablespoon mascarpone cheese, 1 tablespoon sesame oil, butter, 1 tablespoon black sesame seeds, sage, thyme, rosemary, fresh egg pasta, salt and freshly ground black pepper

Filling: Debone the duck thighs and dice the meat; sauté it in butter with the chopped onions and shallots. Add the herbs, salt and pepper. When the meat begins to brown, deglaze with the white wine. When the wine has evaporated complete cooking, adding a little water. Remove the herbs; transfer the meat and pan juices to a food processor and blend with the mascarpone and the Parmigiano Reggiano cheeses. Tortelli: Roll out the pasta, deposit the filling at regular intervals and form the tortelli according to the classic method. Cook in boiling salted water, drain well and transfer to a large sauté pan with a little butter, the sesame oil, the sesame seeds and the strips of glazed tomato. Toss the tortelli with the other ingredients until heated through and serve immediately, garnishing with slices of cooked goose breast and thyme.

Smoked Venison with Polenta and Porcini Mushrooms
Paolo Bellamano

Ingredients for 4 servings:
160 g (5 1/2 oz) very thinly sliced smoked venison cut into 1/2 cm (1/4 inch) strips, 50 g (1 3/4 oz) finely chopped shallots, 50 g (1 3/4 oz) black truffles cut into strips and tossed in a little olive oil, 1 teaspoon chopped black truffle, 2 teaspoons crushed coriander seeds, 2 tablespoons extra virgin olive oil, salt and pepper, 1 teaspoon white truffle oil, 16 porcini mushroom caps, 1 tablespoon mixed chopped herbs (basil, parsley, rosemary, garlic), 4 slices grilled polenta

Place the sliced venison in a bowl and evenly sprinkle the meat with the chopped shallots, chopped black truffle and coriander seeds. Mix the extra virgin olive oil with the truffle oil and drizzle over the venison; mix well.
Grill the mushroom caps seasoning them with the chopped herbs, a little extra olive oil, salt and pepper. Keep warm. Place a slice of grilled polenta in the center of each plate, add a layer of the venison, top with the truffle strips, garnish with 4 mushroom caps and serve. In lieu of the polenta, the venison may be served on a bed wild rocket seasoned with extra virgin olive oil, lemon juice, salt and pepper.

Pitìna with Drunken Cheese
Andrea Bordignon

Ingredients for 4 servings:
260 g (9 oz) pitìna cut into strips, 2 tablespoons extra virgin olive oil, 2 tablespoons vinegar, Treviso endive (or mixed baby greens), salt, drunken cheese from the Lavarino dairy

Arrange a bed of Treviso endive (or mixed greens) on each plate and salt lightly. Sauté the pitìna strips in the extra virgin olive oil over a high flame. Deglaze with the vinegar and allow it to evaporate. Place heaping spoonful of the hot pitìna on each bed of endive and nap with the cooking juices. Top with a very thin slice of the drunken cheese. Accompanied by a Tokaji Fruilano this makes an excellent appetizer. Paired with a Merlot, it may be offered as a second course.

CARPACCIO OF SMOKED BEEF

Vito Boccassini

Ingredients for 4 servings:
280 g (10 oz) smoked beef, 200 g (7 oz) mixed baby greens. Tomato vinaigrette: 3 tomatoes, 30 g (1 oz) extra virgin olive oil, 10 g (2 teaspoons) cider vinegar, salt and pepper. Cucumber quenelles: 2 cucumbers, 10 g (2 teaspoons) cider vinegar, salt and pepper. Tomato quenelles: 3 tomatoes, 30 g (1oz) extra virgin olive oil, fresh oregano flowers, salt and pepper. Goat cheese quenelles: 30 g (1 oz) soft goat cheese, rocket, white pepper.

Prepare the tomato vinaigrette: halve the tomatoes and squeeze out their juice. Emulsify with the extra virgin olive oil, vinegar, salt and pepper. Reserve. Purée the cucumbers in a food processor, transfer the mixture to a strainer and allow it to drain for a few hours. Season the pulp with the vinegar, salt and pepper and reserve. Repeat the process with the tomatoes. Add the chopped rocket and white pepper to the goat cheese and blend well. Thinly slice the beef. Arrange a bed of mixed greens on each plate, lightly salt them and top with slices of the carpaccio. Form tiny quenelles from the cucumber, tomato and goat cheese mixtures and accompany the carpaccio with one of each. Garnish with oregano flowers and drizzle with the tomato vinaigrette.

BEEF CARPACCIO ON A BED OF SPINACH

Maria Rucci

Ingredients for 2 servings:
100 g marinated Jolanda de Colò beef carpaccio, 5 small bunches fresh baby spinach, 150 g (5 1/3 oz) sweet butter, lemon juice, salt and pepper

Wash and trim the spinach leaves, blanch them in boiling salted water and drain well, removing as much water as is possible. Arrange a bed of spinach leaves on each plate and drizzle with the lemon juice. Top with the slices of carpaccio and accompany with a rose of the finest sweet butter and toast.

MARINATED SAN MARCO FILLET WITH CITRUS SAUCE

Angelo Ruatti

Ingredients for 2 servings:
80 g (3 oz) San Marco fillet, 1 bunch watercress, 1 orange peeled and sectioned, juice of 1/2 orange, juice of 1/2 lemon, juice of 1 tangerine, salt, finely ground Sichuan pepper, 100 g (3 1/2 oz) extra virgin olive oil, a few sprigs of wild fennel, julienned zest of 1/2 lemon, julienned zest of 1/2 orange, Beluga caviar

Fillet: Wash and dry the watercress and arrange a bed on each plate. Top with overlapping slices of thinly sliced San Marco fillet and garnish with orange sections. Sprinkle the julienned orange and lemon zests over the fillet and finish with a dollop of caviar.
Citrus Sauce: Emulsify the citrus juices with the extra virgin olive oil, salt and Sichuan pepper until it achieves a medium density. Add the finely chopped wild fennel and drizzle over the San Marco fillet just before serving.

KAISER HAM BUNDLES

Paolo Zoppolati

Ingredients for 4 servings:
20 slices thinly sliced Kaiser ham, 1 carrot, 2 zucchini, 20 baby green beans, 1 garlic clove, 1/2 a small onion, 20 g (3/4 oz) diced pancetta, 2 medium potatoes, extra virgin olive oil, salt, pepper, 50 g (1 3/4) oz freshly grated horseradish, 1 teaspoon chopped chives, 75 ml (3 oz) vegetable broth

Separately blanch the green beans, carrots and zucchini (the latter two cut into strips) in boiling salted water. Drain and refresh in an ice bath. Peel and slice the potatoes; brown them in a non stick pan with a little extra virgin olive oil, the chopped onion and the pancetta cubes. When tender, salt and pepper to taste and divide the potato mixture into 4 equal portions. Form potato cakes and brown well on both sides. Keep warm. Place a zucchini strip, a carrot strip and a green bean on each slice of ham and roll to enclose them. Sauté these bundles in extra virgin olive oil with the garlic clove for 5 minutes. Remove and keep warm. Add the broth, horseradish and chives to the same sauté pan. Reduce and add 1 teaspoon of extra virgin olive oil. Place a potato cake in the center of each plate, top with the ham bundles and nap with the sauce.

SALMON SASHIMI

Luca Nanut

Ingredients for 4 servings:
1 salmon balik, 16 slices pickled ginger, 1 teaspoon wasabi, 4 tablespoons soy sauce, mixed baby greens, soybean sprouts

Slice the balik so as to obtain at least 16 pieces half an inch thick. Arrange a bed of mixed greens on each plate, top with 4 pieces of the salmon and sprinkle with the soybean sprouts. Drizzle each plate with the soy sauce and wasabi taking care not to mix the two. Garnish with the pickled ginger.

SALMON TOAST WITH SMOKED SCAMORZA AND ZUCCHINI

Moreno Cedroni

Ingredients for 4 servings:
330 g (11 1/2 oz) Norwegian smoked salmon, 330 g (11 1/2 oz) zucchini, 100 g (3 1/2 oz) smoked scamorza cheese, parsley, garlic
Sauce: 100 g (3 1/2 oz zucchini), 30 g (1 oz) lemon infused extra virgin olive oil, dash of salt, 50 g (1 3/4 oz) water

Prepare the sauce by emulsifying all of the ingredients in a food processor or blender.
Slice the salmon and then reduce the slices to thin strips. Allow them to marinate with a little extra virgin olive oil, the parsley stems and the garlic. Thinly slice the zucchini crosswise. Slice the cheese to a thickness equal to that of the zucchini. Create four 5 cm (2-inch) circles with the salmon slices on a sheet of baking parchment, top with a layer of overlapping zucchini slices and finish with a layer of cheese. With a spatula slide each prepared circle on to a slice of firm white bread and toast in the oven for a few minutes. Present the "toasts" in shallow bowls, napped with the sauce and topped with a cherry tomato.

CAVIAR CAPPUCCINO

Dario Macorig

Ingredients for 4 servings:
1 kg (2 1/4 lbs) yellow skinned potatoes, 1 teaspoon butter, 2 dl (1 cup) milk, 125 g (approx. 4 1/2 oz) Beluga caviar, 1 container of low fat plain yogurt, chopped chives, salt, pepper

Boil the potatoes in their jackets. When they are fully cooked, peel them and pass them through a ricer. Add the milk, butter, salt and pepper and proceed as you would for classic mashed potatoes. Place a portion of the hot potatoes in the bottom of each of four cups. Top with a dollop of cold yogurt and one of caviar. Sprinkle with chopped chives and serve.

BELUGA STURGEON TARTARE

Emanuele Scarello

Ingredients for 4 servings:
Sturgeon: 400 g (14 oz) smoked wild Beluga sturgeon, 100 g (3 1/2 oz) diced red bell pepper, finely chopped chives, mixed baby greens, Iranian caviar
Vinaigrette: 100 g (3 1/2 oz) grated fresh ginger, 100 g (3 1/2 oz) verjuice, 150 g (5 1/3 oz) extra virgin olive oil, salt and pepper

Emulsify the verjuice, extra virgin olive oil, salt and pepper. Reserve. Dice the sturgeon and mix it with the red pepper and the chives. Arrange a bed of salad greens on each plate, place a portion of the sturgeon tartare in the center and drizzle with the ginger infused vinaigrette.

CAVIAR TOPPED FILLET OF STURGEON ON A BED OF BARLEY — Ernst Knam

Ingredienti per 4 persone:
4 scaloppe di storione di 150 g ciascuna, 250 g orzo perlato, 120 g vino spumante secco, 1 carota, 2 scalogni, 1 cuore di sedano bianco, 1 lt brodo di pesce, olio extra vergine di oliva ligure, erbe assortite (timo, dragoncello, aneto, alloro), 80 g caviale Beluga, sale marino, pepe bianco.

Preparazione:
Sbucciare, lavare e tritare finemente la verdura. Trasferirla in una pentola con poco olio e soffriggere a fuoco basso per circa 5 minuti. Unire le erbe e l'orzo perlato. Rosolare per altri 3 minuti e aggiungere lo spumante. Fare asciugare, salare e pepare. Unire il brodo poco per volta (come se fosse un risotto) e cuocere per circa 30 minuti. Trascorso questo tempo, togliere l'orzo dal fuoco e lasciarlo riposare per almeno 1 ora finché avrà assorbito il brodo e sarà ben gonfiato.

In una padella calda mettere poco olio e cuocere i filetti di storione. Salare e pepare.

Con l'aiuto di un cerchio di circa 12 cm di diametro, sistemare un disco di orzo su ogni piatto, adagiare sopra il filetto di storione, decorare con il caviale Beluga e aggiungere un filo d'olio extra vergine d'oliva. Terminare con poco sale grosso, pepe e un ramo di erbe.

FOIE GRAS AND BROILED ORANGE INFUSED SCAMPI — Mauro Ricciardi

Ingredients for 4 servings:
Salad: Mixed baby greens and herbs such as curly endive, red radicchio, mâche, celery leaves, chive sprigs and edible flowers, extra virgin olive oil, traditional balsamic vinegar of Modena, salt and pepper
Scampi: 12 fresh scampi, 10 g (1 teaspoon) orange powder, 50 g (1 3/4 oz) white bread passed through a sieve and dried in the oven, 50 g (1 3/4 oz) clarified butter, salt and pepper
Foie gras: 400 g (14 oz) foie gras divided into 4 portions, extra virgin olive oil, salt and pepper
Sauce: 2 dl (scant 1 cup) broth made from the scampi heads, 2 teaspoons red wine vinegar, 1 teaspoon traditional balsamic vinegar of Modena, 1 teaspoon sugar, extra virgin olive oil, salt and pepper

Sauce: Clean the scampi eliminating the heads and intestinal vein. Simmer the heads in 2 dl (scant 1 cup) salted water for 15-20 minutes and reserve. Carefully caramelize the sugar in a saucepan, add the strained broth obtained from the scampi heads and deglaze with the two vinegars. Slowly add a drizzle of extra virgin olive oil until the sauce begins to thicken. Reserve.

Scampi: Mix the dried bread with the orange powder. Salt and pepper the scampi tails, dip them in the clarified butter and coat them with the bread/orange mixture. Arrange the scampi on a baking sheet and broil for 3 minutes in a very hot oven, turning them once.

Foie gras: Heat a little extra virgin olive oil in a sauté pan, salt and pepper the slices of foie gras and slip them into the hot oil. Cook them just long enough for them to develop a crisp outer coating while remaining soft and rosy inside.

Presentation: Arrange a bed of mixed greens on each plate; season with a few drops of balsamic vinegar, extra virgin olive oil, salt and pepper. Top with 3 scampi and add a portion of foie gras. Salt and pepper to taste. Heat the reserved sauce if necessary and drizzle over the scampi and foie gras.

GOOSE FOIE GRAS WITH LEMON AND MINT GELATIN — Heinz Beck

Ingredients for 10 servings:
Terrine: 1.5 kg (3 1/3 lbs) goose foie gras, 7.5 cl (1/3 cup) Madeira reduction (prepared according to the classic method), 7.5 cl (1/3 cup) white Port reduction (prepared according to the classic method), 7.5 cl (1/3 cup) white dessert wine, 120 g (4 1/2 oz) thinly sliced lard, salt, freshly ground white pepper
Gelatin: 2 untreated lemons, a few sprigs of mint, 65 g (2 1/4 oz) sugar, 9 g (approx. 2 leaves) sheet gelatin, 7.5 dl (scant 3 1/2 cups) water, salt
Garnish: 40 g (approx. 1 1/2 oz) curly endive, 80 g (approx. 3 oz) mâche (lamb's lettuce), a few sprigs of mint, extra virgin olive oil, salt

Terrine: Separate the lobes of the foie gras, gently open them and remove the veins with tweezers or by hand. It is important not to warm the liver too much while doing this. Transfer the foie gras to a glass dish, dust it with salt and pepper and drizzle with the Madeira and Port reductions as well as the white wine. Allow it to marinate for at least 1 hour in the refrigerator.

Drain the foie gras and arrange the various lobes in a terrine previously lined with slices of lard. Press lightly to eliminate air pockets. Cover and cook in a 70° C (158° F) oven (with the addition of steam) for 50 minutes. Cool the terrine in an ice bath, top with a weight and allow to rest in the refrigerator for 24 hours prior to unmolding.

Gelatin: Wash the lemons and peel them, taking care to remove none of the white pith. Place 5 dl (scant 2 1/4 cups) of water in a saucepan; add half of the lemon zest, the mint and 35 g (1 1/4 oz) of the sugar. Bring to a boil, add the gelatin leaves (previously softened in cold water, the excess pressed out). Strain through a fine sieve and salt if necessary. The gelatin should be dense.

Julienne the remaining lemon zest and boil it in a sugar syrup made from 2.5 dl (1 cup + 2 tablespoons) of water and 30 g (1 oz) of sugar.

Presentation: Unmold the terrine, slice it and cut several 8 cm (3-inch) discs from each slice with a ravioli cutter or similar instrument. Place a disc of terrine on each plate; add a pinch of the julienned lemon zest and nap with a little gelatin. Layer another disc of the terrine and glaze with another veil of gelatin. Garnish with mint leaves fried in extra virgin olive oil and the mixed salad greens seasoned with extra virgin olive oil and salt.

ADDRESSES

The products used in the realization of the receipes were kindly supplied by:

Jolanda de Colò Srl
Via I Maggio 21
33057 Palmanova UD
Tel. 0432-920321
Fax 0432-924664
e-mail: jolandaa@tin.it
www.jolandadecolo.it

Acknowlegements:

Slavko Adamlje
Paolo and Adriano Azzarri
Corrado Barberis
Paolo Bellamano
Dante Bernardis
Paolo, Anna and Angelo Bissolotti
Vito Boccassini
Roberto Bona and Annamaria Lupi
Andrea Bordignon
Gigetto Bortolini
Andrea and Roberto Canton
Sergio Chesani
Daniele Cortiula
Roberto Cozzarolo
Lidia Del Panno and Luigi Damiani
Riccardo De Prà
Vinicio Dovier
Stefano and Marco Fagioli
Philippe Léveillé
Mauro Lorenzon
Delino, Mario and Severino Macor
Dario Macorig
Massimo Maturi and Paolo Razzolini
Sergio Mei
Damiano Miniera
Aldo Morassutti
Luca Nanut
Assunta Palmioli
Mirco Panisson and Massimo Marconi
Damiano Miniera
Giuliana Santagata Pasculli and Maria Rucci
Nicola Perini
Carlo Petrini
Liano Petrozzi and Ida Tondolo
Maurizio Piscini
Germano Pontoni and Bertilla Prevedello
Katrin, Rrak and Zef Prennushi
Enzo Roncati
Angelo Ruatti
Vinicio Sant and Piero Galiano Zanini
Angelo Santificetur
Emanuele Scarello
Alessandro Scian
Mario Suban
Giorgio Travaini and Bruna Anselmi
Anna and Giorgio Tuti
Claudio and Emilio Volpetti
Giuseppe Zoppi and Carlo Gallotti
Ezio and Paolo Zoppolati

RESTAURANTS:

CAFFÉ FLORIAN
30124 Venezia

LOCANDA DELLE TAMERICI
19031 Fiumaretta di Ameglia (Sp)

RISTORANTE AQUILA D'ORO
34070 Dolegna del Collio (Go)

HOTEL RISTORANTE CAMPIELLO
33048 San Giovanni al Natisone (Ud)

RISTORANTE DA GIGETTO
31050 Miane (Tv)

RISTORANTE DEL DOGE
33033 Codroipo (Ud)

ALBERGO RISTORANTE DOLADA
32010 Plois di Pieve d'Alpago (Bl)

RISTORANTE LA TERAZZA - HOTEL FOUR SEASONS
20121 Milano

RISTORANTE KURSAAL
33020 Sauris di Sotto (Ud)

RISTORANTE LÀ DI PETROS
33030 frazione Mels di Colloredo di Monte Albano (Ud)

RISTORANTE LA MADONNINA DEL PESCATORE
60019 Marzocca di Senigallia (An)

RISTORANTE LA PERGOLA - CAVALIERI HILTON
00136 Roma

ALBERGO RISTORANTE LA PRIMULA
33080 San Quirino (Pn)

RISTORANTE LA TAVERNA
Colloredo di Monte Albano (Ud)

RISTORANTE MAFFEI
37121 Verona

RISTORANTE MAXIM
Ljubljana (Slovenia)

RISTORANTE MIRAMONTI L'ALTRO
25062 Concesio loc. Costorio (Bs)

OSTERIA DEL TRENO
20124 Milano

TAVERNA DELLA TRISA
20145 Milano

RISTORANTE VILLA CARAFA
70031 Andria (Ba)

RISTORANTE VILLA TORRE QUADRA
70034 Bitonto (Ba)

TRATTORIA AGLI AMICI
33100 Udine

TRATTORIA AL GIARDINETTO
34071 Cormons (Go)

TRATTORIA BLASUT
33050 Lavariano di Mortegliano (Ud)

TRATTORIA DA TONI
33030 Gradiscutta di Varmo (Ud)

ANTICA TRATTORIA SUBAN
34128 Trieste

TRATTORIA VIA VAI
26010 Bolzone di Ripalta Cremasca (Cr)

CATERERS:

LA NUOVA ARTE DEL CATERING
20135 Milano

WINE BARS:

ENOTECA CATULLO
26100 Cremona

ENOTECA DAMIANI
25049 Iseo (Bs)

ENOITECA LA CANEVA
30016 Jesolo (Ve)

ENOTECA LA SOSTA DEL ROSSELLINO
50135 Firenze

ENOTECA NANUT
34121 Trieste

ENOTECA ONOFRI
06031 Bevagna (Pg)

DELICATESSENS:

GASTRONOMIA AZZARRI
50125 Firenze

GASTRONOMIA CONVIVIUM FIRENZE
50126 Firenze

GASTRONOMIA IL SALUMAIO
15100 Alessandria

GASTRONOMIA IL SALUMAIO
70122 Bari

GASTRONOMIA LA CORTE DI MONTENAPOLEONE
20121 Milano

GASTRONOMIA PANISSON
30121 Venezia

GASTRONOMIA SPECK
34121 Trieste

GASTRONOMIA VOLPETTI
Quartiere Testaccio, 00153 Roma

GASTRONOMIA ZOPPI & GALLOTTI
20122 Milano

CHEFS:

GERMANO PONTONI
33037 Pasian di Prato (Ud)

VINICIO DOVIER - VIROCA
33010 Feletto Umberto, Tavagnacco (Ud)